The Experiences of Ghanaian Live-in Caregivers in the United States

The Experiences of Ghanaian Live-in Caregivers in the United States

Martha Donkor

LEXINGTON BOOKS
Lanham • Boulder • New York • London

Published by Lexington Books
An imprint of The Rowman & Littlefield Publishing Group, Inc.
4501 Forbes Boulevard, Suite 200, Lanham, Maryland 20706
www.rowman.com

Unit A, Whitacre Mews, 26-34 Stannary Street, London SE11 4AB

British Library Cataloguing in Publication Information Available

Library of Congress Cataloging-in-Publication Data Available
Names: Donkor, Martha, author.
Title: The experiences of Ghanaian live-in caregivers in the United States / Martha Donkor.
Description: Lanham : Lexington Books, 2017. | Includes bibliographical references and index.
Identifiers: LCCN 2017047426 (print) | LCCN 2017047836 (ebook) | ISBN 9781498564465 (ebook) | ISBN 9781498564458 (cloth : alk. paper)
Subjects: LCSH: Women caregivers—United States. | Women immigrants—United States. | Foreign workers, Ghanaian—United States. | Ghanaians—United States.
Classification: LCC HD6072.2.U5 (ebook) | LCC HD6072.2.U5 D66 2017 (print) | DDC 331.76164980820973—dc23
LC record available at https://lccn.loc.gov/2017047426

∞™ The paper used in this publication meets the minimum requirements of American National Standard for Information Sciences—Permanence of Paper for Printed Library Materials, ANSI/NISO Z39.48-1992.

Printed in the United States of America

Contents

List of Tables vii
Preface ix
Acknowledgments xvii

1 Women, Globalization, Migration, and Work 1
2 Ghana in the Global Political Economy 13
3 Ghanaian Women and the International Migration Process 31
4 The Chance and Choice of Live-in Caregiving 47
5 The Dynamics of Live-in Caregiving 71
6 Organizing Family from a Distance 95
7 Live In at What Cost? 109
8 Rethinking Immigrant Women's Care Work 119

Bibliography 125
Index 139
About the Author 143

List of Tables

Table 2.1	Representation of Women in Selected Parliaments, 1960–2017	25
Table 2.2	Cabinet Positions held by Women, 6th and 7th Parliaments of the 4th Republic	26
Table 3.1	Ghanaian Immigrant Arrivals to Canada and the US, 1979–1985	41
Table 3.2	Ghanaian Immigrant Arrivals to Canada and the US, 1986–1992	42
Table 4.1	The Ten Fastest-Growing Jobs, 2012–2022	52

Preface

The migration of women and the work they do as migrants has been the subject of extensive research. Given the scope of the research, there is not a single trope that adequately captures the range of experiences that women go through in their various destinations as immigrant workers. In spite of that, there seems to be a community, if you will, of global immigrant women who can be identified by their concentration in domestic care work. Their countries of origin, the circumstances of their migration, their destinations, and the types of domestic work they engage in may differ, but study after study portrays these women in terms that emphasize common vulnerabilities and victimhood in wealthy metropolises around the world. When placed within a larger context, the situation of immigrant domestic workers epitomizes in microcosm the unequal relations that exist between wealthy and poor countries, relations that began with the processes of colonialism and now manifest in the form of capitalist globalization. Exploitation and accumulation undergirded colonialism, and continues to drive capitalist globalization, although the paths taken were/are somewhat different. For instance, colonialist exploitation involved members of wealthy nations going to poor countries to extract wealth; in capitalist globalization, people from poor countries, in this case women, go to wealthy nations so that their resource—labor—can be extracted and exploited. Capitalist globalization thus extends what I term "patriarchal benevolence" to women from poor countries. That is, in the process of exploitation, women are given the opportunity, through migration, to acquire resources that they would not have acquired otherwise, so that exploitation that is inherent in the relationship between globalization and migration is masked. But even as we consider the exploitative nature of capitalist globalization with regard to migrant women's work as domestic caregivers, we should note that women have not been passive victims of their exploitation.

They have acted within the exploitative structures[1] to satisfy goals they have defined for themselves. I use the experiences of Ghanaian immigrant women care workers in New York City to tease out some of the complexities associated with globalization, migration, and women's agency in the face of their exploitation in foreign lands.

The choice of Ghanaian women is deliberate. Ghana[2] epitomizes the colonial-independent-neo-colonial state whose citizens have responded to the negative impact of capitalist exploitation by migrating to countries of relative economic advantage. Britain, the colonial master, encouraged Ghana (as it did with its other colonies) to produce primary goods for an export market in which Ghana did not have the privilege or right to price its goods. Ghana produced and exported cocoa, timber, and minerals, notably gold, to Britain and imported British-manufactured wares whose prices had already been determined at source. That unequal global trade continued after independence when Ghana expanded its trading partner base but was still unable to have the power to price its goods on the international market in the new phase of global capitalism.[3] Ghana found itself competing in a global political economy at a competitive disadvantage. The poverty that resulted, coupled with political mismanagement, created conditions that were conducive to mass migration. Women were active in the migration process, constituting slightly less than 50% of Ghanaian migrants who settled in the US prior to 2010.[4] A significant minority of the women entered domestic care service. Yet, the literature on immigrant care workers in the US does not acknowledge the Ghanaian women's contribution to and experience of care work due to the heavy focus on women from Asia, the Caribbean, and Latin America. My interest here is not to assign reasons for the oversight. My goal is to incorporate the experiences of the Ghanaian women into the body of literature on domestic care work in the US for a richer and more complete body of knowledge.

SCOPE OF THE BOOK

I started research for this book in 2009. I had applied for and was awarded a Faculty Professional Development Council grant from the Pennsylvania State System of Higher Education (PASSHE) to research the work experiences of Ghanaian immigrant women in the US. I decided to focus on women who did live-in caregiving. At the time of the award, an increasing number of Ghanaian women living in Toronto, Canada, who I had known during my doctoral research days were moving down to the US to do live-in or going back to school to become personal support workers. The Ghanaian women living in major cities in northeastern US, especially in New York and Newark, took jobs as live-in caregivers and passed on word to their friends about openings for those who would be interested. Surely something special was happening within the domestic care sector for the Ghanaian women, but what was it? My intention was to find that out. At the same time I wondered whether or not the women were aware of the negative descriptions of the job conditions and if that meant anything to them. Why would they choose a job sector that exploited and impoverished women, as per expert opinion? How did the women see domestic work? How would they organize their own families (if they were married and/or with children) if they live away from home? What would be the nature of their social life? Importantly, how did their work fit analytically with discourse on women's work that uses the double day as a conceptual framework?

These were not new questions, but asking a group of women who have not been studied as domestic workers in a sector of domestic work that is becoming popular but also under-studied brings fresh perspectives that deepen our understanding of immigrant women's work as caregivers. What emerged from my study was that some of the conclusions previously drawn about immigrant care workers were over-generalized in at least two areas. Undervaluation and exploitation, two major concepts that have dominated discourse on care work, did not seem to apply to the women I studied. The women did not believe that their work was undervalued; similarly, they were equally positioned to potentially exploit their employers in material ways. These conclusions stem from the kind of domestic work that the women were engaged in. They took care of people who were mostly middle-class white men who wanted to live in the comfort of their homes to be cared for by private caregivers instead of going to retirement homes when they could no longer manage the basics of daily living. This type of live-in caregiving is different from other domestic arrangements where workers live in households of multiple family members; it is also different from care work in which women work in assisted living facilities and join their own families at the end of the workday. The type of care work that the women performed is steadily gaining popularity among caregivers, although compared with people who care for children, for example, it constitutes a small component of the caregiving industry. Nonetheless, it is the type of care work that Ghanaian immigrant women are attracted to. And for good reason: they believe that their type has more prestige and pays better than other forms of care work.

The women called their work "private practice," a rather suggestive name but one that captured the dynamics of their work conditions. Many of them did not get their jobs through an employment agency and none got theirs through government programs that allow caregivers to enter the US on special visas to work as domestics. In fact, the women did not immigrate to the US specifically to work as caregivers. Rather, they migrated as economic migrants and took advantage of a job sector that had openings for them and which they thought satisfied their economic needs. Most of the women got their jobs by first working as live-out caregivers with employment agencies; once they had worked with particular persons for some time they would make private arrangements with the care recipients and then move in. A few were placed by agencies. From these humble beginnings private practice expanded in the Ghanaian community in New York City and the surrounding areas.

The very private nature of the negotiation that women entered into with care recipients might suggest that they could be susceptible to the exploitation and victimizations that have characterized major studies of immigrant live-in care work. As we will see later in the book, the women's agency and self-assurance ensured that their clients did not take undue advantage of them. Another significant thing to note about the women was that they did not believe that they were pushed into domestic care work as a result of endemic racism in American society. They were pragmatic in their expectations of jobs that could be available to them as immigrant women of color and decided on domestic caregiving. Settling into private practice was easy for the women since they did not require any kind of training, unlike child care and other palliative care that require caregivers to have some type of certification.

The women's stories also explicate an inchoate and nuanced discourse on immigrant domestic care work that reflects the convergence of globalization and local politics and their impact on women. Poverty can sometimes produce individual irresponsibility, but when irresponsibility takes on a national character, it results in collective hurt. Globalization certainly affected politics in Ghana and created severe hardships on women. This cultural and political background influenced the women's perceptions of care work. We can assume that the Ghanaian women's work conditions as domestic workers were similar to the work conditions of immigrant women from other parts of the world. What we do not know is how they responded to those conditions. I argue that their background shaped their responses to their work conditions.

I also use the Ghanaian women to explore the historical link that African American women had to domestic work and the possibility that African immigrant women, as black women, were circumscribed in their job options because of their race and gender. Works by leading African American feminist scholars like Judith Rollins, Paula Giddings, and Darlene Clarke Hine show that African American women did domestic work because they had limited avenues to other forms of paid employment.[5] The authors also show that when other, more "respectable" job opportunities opened up, African American women left domestic service. My goal here was to tease out any historical continuities in domestic work that are defined by race, gender, class, and the Ghanaian women's understanding of that historical link. What emerged was that the Ghanaian women did not see their work as less respectable to make them want to leave for other "respectable" jobs.

Researching the lives of the Ghanaian women was at once exciting and frustrating. It was exciting because I got women's direct perspectives of their work. Because nobody had studied Ghanaian women in "private practice," I had to talk to them directly for information. Doing so gave the women the chance to speak for themselves instead of getting their perspectives refracted through other sources. It was at the point of doing interviews that the process became frustrating. I had initially anticipated that I would take about eight months to locate women, arrange interview schedules, and then conduct the interviews. It soon became apparent that I would not be able to visit them at their places of work. Nor could I interview them during work hours in the day. This suggested that live-in was less flexible for women in private practice. In the end, what was supposed to be face-to-face interviews over an eight-month period became a series of nighttime phone interviews and a few face-to-face interviews that extended over eighteen months. Of the thirty women that I interviewed, only four were able to grant face-to-face interviews. Four abandoned the interviews half way. Thus, the data presented in this book is based on interviews conducted with twenty-six women. The women, ranging in age from twenty-four to fifty-seven years, had done this kind of work for an average of ten years. In terms of education, only one woman said that she held a master's degree in education. One was a trained teacher and had several years of elementary teaching experience. The rest were literate with varying degrees of pre-tertiary academic achievement. Only four of the women were not married; three were divorced, and the remaining nineteen were married, some with adult children who did not need immediate care, some had young children in Ghana while still others had their children and spouses living together in the US. In terms of legal status, with the exception of four women who were on visitor's visas, all the women were naturalized citizens or green card holders who had lived in the country for an average of fifteen years. In addition to the women, I also interviewed three men whose wives did live-in caregiving for their perspectives on the job and family dynamics. A young man whose mother did live-in when he was growing up later withdrew from the study.

Organization of the Book

The increased migration of women from poor regions to more affluent centers in recent decades can be attributed to the convergence of globalization and local dynamics. Thus chapter 1 analyzes globalization and its link to women's migration. It also examines the "double day" as a framework that explains the family-work tension and how live-in caregivers fit (or don't fit) in that mode of analysis. The chapter posits that although married immigrant caregivers face the same kinds of challenges that married non-caregiver women face in the family, immigrant caregivers devised different strategies based on what I term "triple management" to deal with the work-family conflict. Ghana debuted in the global economy not as a country but as independent chiefdoms, kingdoms, and small communities, and then progressed into a colonial entity that finally gained independence as a modern state. Chapter 2 gives a brief historical overview of these transitions to situate the analysis within the framework of globalization, especially as it affected Ghana in the last three decades of the twentieth century. The central point of the chapter is that 1979 and 1981 were watershed periods in Ghana's history that had their roots deep in the history of the economic and political evolution of Ghana. The events of 1979 and 1981 created conditions conducive for mass migration which, for the first time, involved large numbers of women. The migration of the women was fraught with difficulty. Simple processes such as obtaining a passport could ruin the ambitions of a potential migrant. Women endured gender-specific hardships and winding passages through several countries until they finally settled in the US. Chapter 3 explores these dynamics and sets up the stage for us to appreciate women's work choices once they settled in the US.

In 2009 when I started interviewing the women, the domestic work sector was growing even as the market crashed and thousands of people lost their jobs. In the midst of the economic chaos, the Ghanaian women were gainfully employed, suggesting that the domestic work sector withstood the economic downturn. Importantly, something had to explain why the Ghanaian women selected home care beyond the sector's ability to withstand the vagaries of the economy. Chapter 4 explores the women's decisions to do live-in and concludes that live-in served the dual purpose of giving the women financial capital and as escape for women with certain kinds of problems. Chapter 5 puts the women's narratives of caregiving at center stage. The women explain what they did, their wages, relationship with employers, and what they thought about their work in an effort to assess their sense of exploitation and undervaluation that has characterized both social and academic discourse on caregiving. The central argument of the chapter is that the women's narratives challenge some of the long-held conclusions about care work as undervalued and exploitative.

Using triple management as an explanatory model, chapter 6 examines the creative ways in which women interacted with the multiple family structures they belonged to from a distance. Migration created hybridized family forms that women related to as a means to maintain social presence and a sense of identity and belonging. Triple management, which refers to the organizational and managerial strategies that women adopted to maintain relationships with multiple family forms, offers a model of explanation that encapsulates the transnational nature of the women's families. Like every type of care work, private practice posed familial and structural problems that women encountered as they performed their duties. Chapter 7 takes a look at some of these problems with particular emphasis on long-term problems regarding old-age financial insecurity and poverty. Chapter 7 draws the attention of the women to rethink private practice as a long-term job choice. The concluding chapter briefly relates private practice to selected theories on immigrant care work.

The book is written mainly as a historical narrative that allows women to "speak" where appropriate so that their voices are heard. It also exhibits a truly transnational character by linking the women's lives in Ghana to their decisions in the US to underscore the dynamism of globalization in the lives of immigrant women. Ultimately, the book makes the case that the Ghanaian women judged the worth of their work more in terms of their ability to be financially independent and have leverage in their families and communities in Ghana and less in terms of how American society viewed care work. What I hope this book will achieve is to use the Ghanaian women's voices to draw attention to the need for us to consider cultural differences and agency in the ways that immigrant women interpret their work conditions. The opportunity to immigrate and the challenges of work in a different cultural and political context can elicit complex responses from women that may make generalizations somehow risky. The Ghanaian women's stories suggest that long-held assumptions about immigrant women's care work can create a mirror reflection that describes how "we" see care work versus how "they" see it.

NOTES

1. Meryl Altman and Kerry Pannell, "Policy Gaps and Theory Gaps: Women and Migrant Domestic Labor," *Feminist Economics* 18, no. 2 (April 2012): 292.
2. I use Ghana throughout this chapter to refer to the geographical region that eventually became the modern-day state of Ghana to avoid the confusion of using names for the different peoples that inhabited the region before British colonization, and then after colonization to shift between the colonial and modern name.
3. Kwadwo Konadu-Agyemang, "The Best of Times and the Worst of Times: Structural Adjustment Programs and Uneven Development in Africa: The Case of Ghana," *Professional Geographer* 52, no. 3 (2000): 471.
4. Konadu-Agyeman, "The Best of Times," 471.
5. Judith Rollins, Between Women: *Domestics and their Employers* (Philadelphia: Temple University Press, 1985); Paula Giddings, When and Where I Enter: The Impact of Black Women on Race and Sex in America (Toronto: Bantam Book, 1985); Darlene Clarke Hine, ed., *Hine Sight: Black Women and the Reconstruction of American History* (Brooklyn, NY: Carlson Publishing, 1994).Acknowledgments

Acknowledgments

This manuscript would not have been possible without the invaluable help I received from people I know, those I met casually, and others I did not meet but whose contributions made this a success. I would first like to acknowledge the members of the Faculty Professional Development Council of the Pennsylvania State System of Higher Education for awarding the grant that made the research possible. In this regard, I extend my gratitude to Drs. Naod Kebede and Peter Lindeman of Edinboro University of Pennsylvania as local chairs of the grant at the time of the award, and Ms. Linda Lacny for her useful suggestions during the initial stages of writing the proposal. I'd also like to thank my colleague and friend Dr. Joan Woolfrey and my brother Dr. Obed Mfum-Mensah for their encouragement and support. I extend my deepest appreciation to Dr. Clara Benneh and Dr. Darko Opoku for their help. Many thanks to Suzzy for taking care of the house when I was "too busy" to lend a hand. I also thank the anonymous reviewers and editors for making it all possible. To the brave women and men who shared their lives' experiences, I reserve my greatest gratitude. I dedicate this book to them for their selflessness, cooperation, and enthusiasm as they told their stories to a total stranger. It takes courage to trust a stranger with personal information. For that I say thanks, fellow immigrants.

Chapter 1

Women, Globalization, Migration, and Work

Movement of people[1] within or outside national borders attracts scholarly interest, and for good reason. People must have compelling reasons to leave the familiarity of their homes to go to new places, even if temporarily. Scholars have used a push-pull framework to explain why people will migrate and why they will end up in certain places and not others.[2] One of the fundamental motivations that undergird individual decisions to migrate is economic opportunity and security elsewhere. Of course economic opportunity elsewhere suggests economic hardship at home. Phenomena such as natural disasters, wars, environmental degradation, or poor government policies can create economic hardship, especially for vulnerable members of society. The ability of individuals to cope with such phenomena determines whether or not they will migrate. Coping means that there are resources, individual or societal, that people can access in such situations to ease hardships associated with an event. For instance, Hurricane Katrina, one of the most powerful hurricanes in the US history, hit the Gulf Coast in 2005 and caused a heavy toll in human life and property damage. By 2010, one of the worst affected cities, New Orleans, was all but rehabilitated, and residents who moved out as a result of the hurricane had come back home. Contrast that with an earthquake that hit Haiti in 2010 that also caused heavy human casualties and property damage. Five years later, in 2015, thousands of displaced Haitians were living in tents, waiting and hoping that they would be resettled elsewhere.[3] If these people had the resources, they probably would leave that difficult life behind; however, because of the lack of resources, they have been internally displaced and may continue to live like that for a long time. At a glance one can say that these events are not comparable because of the social, economic, and political contexts in which they occurred. But that precisely is the point of the comparison. It is made to underscore the fact that context matters in events that cause people to migrate, and that migration forced by economic hardship generally moves in one direction—from impoverished areas to well-resourced regions.

Despite the fact that economic hardship affects both men and women, for a long time the historiography on international migration proceeded as a male phenomenon. The assumption was that men migrated and women stayed back to take care of the family. When women migrated, it was because the men in their lives migrated.[4] Recent scholarship has debunked that view and has emphasized that women have migrated as independent migrants. They have responded to economic hardship just like men. Women have traveled from rural to urban areas in their own countries or crossed international boundaries in search of better economic opportunities based on their own decisions and not those made by the men in their lives.[5] In more recent years analyses of women's migration, local and international, has been done largely within the framework of globalization.[6] Thus it is important to examine the contours of the discourse on globalization and its relation to women's migration and work.

GLOBALIZATION AND MIGRATION

As a word and phenomenon globalization has become a buzzword in academia, the business world, and the global political economy. As a word, globalization has defied scholarly consensus on its definition and origin. In terms of definition, scholars have largely explained or described rather than define globalization. Pat and Hugh Armstrong, for example, describe globalization as a process through which the world is brought closer together as a result of the activities of transnational corporations (TNCs).[7] Others, like Allan Ssenyonga simply see globalization as Americanization, a reflection of America's global reach in the economic, cultural, and military realms.[8] According to Breny Mendoza, globalization in Western popular usage means "[the] unprecedented interconnectedness between countries and peoples that has grown out of the spread of capitalism, the fall of socialism, the existence of the internet and the new information and communications technologies."[9] In simple terms, globalization describes a world in flux, fueled by tremendous flows of capital, people, and technology that promise progress to all caught in its ambit.

In the same way that scholars do not speak with a common voice on the definition of globalization, so also do they not agree on its origin. One of the earliest debates in this wise occurred between the late British sociologist and political theorist Paul Hirst and another British international relations professor David Held. Held and Hirst both agreed that the global economy has undergone tremendous transformation; however, they diverged on when the transformation began. Hirst pointed to the end of World War II as the beginning of changes to the global economy due to the failure of Germany to build on the momentum created by a wartime economy.[10] By doing so, Hirst suggested that globalization is a fairly recent phenomenon. Held, on the other hand, placed the origin of globalization earlier than the 1940s by arguing that it was rather the culmination of processes of colonialism and imperialism that began in the nineteenth century. Held's view is shared by other experts including Rainer Tetzlaff.[11]

As a phenomenon, globalization is best perceived in terms of its impact. People in the corporate world admire it for its promise of economic prosperity and global development. Activists from diverse and sometimes divergent backgrounds are united in their hatred of globalization for its negative impact on women, indigenous peoples, and the environment. Nationalists express concern over globalization's threat to national boundaries and security, while feminists lament its creation of a bifurcated world defined by inequality between countries of the global North and South and women in both spheres caught in varying degrees of opportunities and disadvantages.[12] As Mendoza has observed, globalization has created a world economy in which "only territorial points that are saturated by global forces such as zones with intense traffic of migrants, global assembly lines, finance capital flows … acquire a real social, political and economic significance."[13] It is this nebulous, overarching quality of globalization that has thrown the question of its ownership into confusion and set groups of activists against it as a phenomenon.

Feminist scholars, especially those working from a transnational perspective, take the view that globalization hurts Third World women, notwithstanding the potential advantages that the Third World generally might enjoy by participating in new markets and new technologies made possible by the internet revolution. However, there are analysts who counter the feminist position by arguing that TNCs, in particular, benefit Third World countries in which they operate by creating opportunities for workers to earn higher incomes to be able to purchase and consume high-quality goods and services.[14] The problem with this kind of praise of the impact of globalization on Third World countries is the narrow lens through which it views the impact. There is a lot more to capitalist globalization than the presence of TNCs in certain Third World countries. Whatever benefits Third World countries derive from globalization are mediated by import and export controls, pricing of primary goods on the international market, debt servicing, and the programs of the Bretton Woods Institutions. Thus the emphasis on the benefits of TNCs to Third World countries at the exclusion of other powerful influences is a myopic view of a complex phenomenon.

Moreover, less emphasized but significant are the racist ideologies that drive the programming of TNCs in Third World countries. Just as in colonial times European nations pursued racist policies in order to exploit colonized subjects, so also have contemporary wealthy nations that control global capital used racist strategies to exploit Third World countries to further enrich themselves. The well-documented activities of TNCs best illustrate the point. These include their disregard for safety standards at work sites in Third World countries where they operate; the siphoning of local resources—human and natural—without embarking on development projects to replace what they have taken; the appallingly low wages they pay workers; the pollution of bodies of water through improper disposal of industrial waste; and the pollution of the environment by spewing dangerous fumes and gases into the atmosphere.[15] These are practices that will not be *tolerated* in the first world countries where the TNCs originate and are headquartered. In Third World countries, TNCs pursue accumulation with impunity because in most cases, governments of those countries rely on these large corporations for their own existence. Industrial accidents like a fire that broke out in a Bangladeshi garment factory and killed over a hundred workers in 2012 are fairly common where TNCs operate.[16] The last time an industrial accident of that kind occurred in the US was in 1911, more than a hundred years ago. TNCs stifle the growth of local industries and then repatriate their profits, leaving people who had previously supported themselves and their families through traditional, local industries in unbearable economic situations while the meager wages they pay workers do not go far. No wonder one scholar concluded that colonialism and globalization are two sides of the same coin.[17]

Similarly, the Bretton Woods institutions which are important props of capitalist globalization pursue programs that hurt more than they help Third World countries.[18] The World Bank and the International Monetary Fund (IMF) advance loans and technical advice to Third World countries to ensure economic development. The development models the financial institutions use are based on models used in advanced Western economies where market forces determine the direction and health of the economy. The loans they advance to implement development projects carry heavy interests. Their approach of applying Western standards to Third World economies again mimics the attitudes and strategies that colonialists adopted toward non-Western peoples. The colonialists imposed their cultural and economic motifs on people who they described as backward and uncivilized and needing redemption from themselves simply because those people were different from the Europeans.[19] IMF and World Bank programs have had similar effects. Structural adjustment programs (SAPs) provide a good example of such impositions. Kwadwo

Konadu-Agyemang, a demographic geographer who studied SAPs in Ghana states:

> According to neoclassical economic theory that forms the bedrock of World Bank and IMF restructuring programs, socioeconomic and spatial inequalities are merely short-term aberrations that arise from structural factors, in an otherwise well functioning system. Consequently, it is assumed that the inequalities created between the rich and the poor and between prosperous and depressed areas melt away as countries undertake development programs, especially those that are driven by market forces.[20]

Since IMF and World Bank development programs are imposed on so-called developing nations, it suggests that the financial institutions presume to know what is wrong with these nations better than the nations know about themselves. Not much has changed from the shift from colonialism to capitalist globalization in the global political economy. Jana Everett and Sue Ellen Charlton, authors of *Women in a Globalizing World*, state that SAPs have deleterious effects on recipient countries and their citizens.[21] These financial institutions lend money to developing nations within a framework of neo-liberal econometrics that require less government involvement and intervention in the economy to achieve economies of scale. Less government involvement means cuts in social programs including education and health care, freeze on government hiring and large-scale layoff of a sizable portion of those already employed.[22] SAPs are ineffectual in countries where government is the biggest employer and the private sector is less developed. In such countries, a freeze on hiring means unemployment, especially for new college graduates; and layoffs not only lead to immediate unemployment for previously employed individuals but also negatively affect their retirement entitlements.

These outcomes of globalization, whether emanating from the activities of TNCs or the international financial institutions, are not gender neutral. Women tend to suffer disproportionately due to their already marginal social and economic positions. To elucidate with just one example, women constitute a greater percentage of people who derive their livelihood directly from the land in developing nations. Women are the primary producers of food; they also provide firewood and water; and raise small animals for consumption and for local markets. When the environment is degraded all these aspects of women's lives are negatively affected. Women may walk long distances to fetch firewood and water,[23] be unable to generate income from traditional sources, work longer and harder to meet the needs of their families, etc. Women who are employed by TNCs, especially in the garment industry, face challenging situations. They work longer hours in sub-standard conditions only to be paid wages that cannot support them and their families.[24] And when the corporations relocate, for whatever reason, and unemployment hits a family, it is usually the women who must sacrifice in order to keep families together.[25] Similarly, SAPs negatively affect women because of their roles as nurturers and caregivers. Women who depend on government services for children and disabled family members or on the salaries of employed husbands will find themselves shorn of the services and deprived of their husbands' incomes when government services are cut and husbands are laid off due to IMF and World Bank conditionalities. When Ghana's economy tanked in the early 1980s and a severe drought and bush fires destroyed farms, I witnessed women's sacrifices for their families firsthand. My aunt would put water on fire to give the children the assurance that food would be ready soon; then she would go out to queue for rice or cassava powder. By the time she would be ready to prepare food, the firewood would be burned out and she had to restart the fire. She would usually wait for the children to eat, and when there was none left, tell the children that once they were full, she was going to be full too. Women ate less, slept less, worked harder and longer, and suffered poor health as a consequence. People referred to their prominent collar bones as "wearing Rawlings' chain."

Interestingly, globalization also enhances people's chances to migrate. Because globalization increases information dissemination, people are able to learn about places and the opportunities these places offer. And improvements in transportation make it easier for potential migrants to travel from rural areas to urban centers in the same country or for those who have the financial resources to look further afield to international destinations in hopes of improving their lives. Not surprisingly, women have taken advantage of these opportunities to travel to areas of economic promise. This female migratory pattern tends to be unidirectional, gravitating mainly from poor countries to affluent ones as unskilled and semi-skilled workers or professionals in several areas of expertise. But as we will see later, the migration of women from Third World countries to developed countries such as the US is not without its own challenges. And yet when they finally enter these first world spaces, women encounter problems that make their situation seem like they have come full circle. The kinds of employment opportunities that are open to many Third World may not seem like jobs that will improve their economic situations, which is the reason why they migrated in the first place.

Conceptualizing Immigrant Women's Work

In thinking about immigrant women's work, it is important to place the analysis within the larger context of women and work and to examine how certain discursive tropes bear on immigrant women's work specifically. In this regard it is also important to examine the double day (or as Arlie Hochschild calls it, the "second shift")[26] as a framework that explains the tension that exists between women's remunerative labor and domestic responsibilities. Domestic responsibility is at the center of discourse on the double day, and domestic work is also work that is principally associated with immigrant women's remunerative labor; hence it is imperative to analyze the linkages between immigrant women's work and the double day to understand how "immigrantness" affects the definition of "woman" in relation to work.

The double day describes the situation where a woman works a full-time job for pay and then goes home to take full charge of domestic responsibilities and chores. Arlie Russell Hochschild, for instance, has clearly shown that work and family are interrelated and that women's success in the former depends largely on how they manage the latter.[27] From cooking to cleaning, nursing the young, the aged, and the sick, to organizing other aspects of family life, women have a full schedule at home. This full schedule, when coupled with full-time work, can affect women's output and chance of upward mobility at their places of work. This is what Misra, Lundquist, and Templer found in their study of faculty at the University of Massachusetts, Amherst. They discovered that female and male faculty generally worked equally long hours; however, female faculty with childcare responsibilities at home spent less time on research in order to devote full attention to teaching, mentoring, and service. The strategic apportionment of time meant that the women were able to satisfy student and university needs and requirements but jeopardized their own chances of promotion in an institution that placed much emphasis on research as a condition for promotion.[28]

The difficulties of managing work and family life was recently re-popularized by Anne-Marie Slaughter, one time Director of Policy Planning in the Obama administration. When she quit that job she wrote an op-ed in the *Atlantic Monthly* in which she explained that she left her prestigious position partly because of terms governing sabbaticals at Princeton University, where she was a faculty member, and partly due to the difficulty of fulfilling her role as mother to a teenaged son.[29] Following that article, Elizabeth Vargas, a 20/20 news anchor, organized a women's focus group on the Oprah Show to talk about the impact of family life on women's careers. The women who participated in the discussion emphasized that they were affected, to varying degrees, by the family-work dynamic and revealed the difficult choices that they must make in their efforts to work and have families at the same time.

As powerful as the discussion was in capturing the dilemmas that women face as workers and family members, the analytical and theoretical underpinning of the double day weakens when we consider that some women rely on other women to get their domestic chores done. Importantly, the double day assumes that women go home or should go home at the end of the work day to assume domestic responsibilities. However, this is not always the case.

Live-in caregivers do not have the privilege of going home at the end of each workday to take care of their families. And yet in soap operas and on the silver screen we see these domestic workers as savvy, reliable, always available, sometimes powerful (because of their knowledge of family secrets) house helps whose singular purpose appears to be the welfare of the families they work for. This portrayal of domestic work in popular culture is an interesting contradiction in that it is simultaneously accurate and inaccurate. While showing the women's dedication to their work, the women are not portrayed as people who might have families of their own. Their portrayal as isolated individuals in the private homes of their employers distorts their real-life situations because, in most cases, they have families with similar needs as the ones they care for. Thus, embedding immigrant women's work within a discourse on women and work that uses the double day as a conceptual framework reveals the complexity of its analytical applicability as well as its fracturing of the category woman.

Live-in caregivers have a complicated relationship with work and family. They must care for their families in the same way as other women care for theirs—show affection, nurture, organize, and manage. Yet unlike other women, most live-in caregivers are immigrants, and that adds another layer to the complexity of their lives in relation to caring for their families. They have dependents in both the original country and the destination country that they must care for in addition to the care they give for pay. Hochschild describes this aspect of immigrant women's lives as "global care chains."[30] Given the complexity of care work as it relates to immigrant women's lives as family women, I suggest an analysis of care work within a framework of triple management to capture the layered responsibility that caregivers face taking care of their own immediate families, cultivating relationships in the immigrant community, and staying connected to the family left in the old country from a distance. Triple management is also used as a conceptual and analytical framework to capture the complex dynamic of juggling three families at different sites at the same time and still maintain a positive outlook toward work. As we will see later, the Ghanaian women did not necessarily see the demands of care work and familial responsibility in tension with each other, in the sense that the double day suggests.

An aspect of care work that has dominated the discursive landscape has been the work conditions. Scholars generally paint a not so attractive picture of conditions surrounding domestic care work. Whether they care for children, elderly persons, or persons with disabilities in institutionalized or private settings, care workers handle bodies that are mostly vulnerable and usually subject to bodily functions that may be considered "dirty and disgusting."[31] Women's supposed qualities for empathy and sensitivity are believed to make them naturally suited to handle such mess; yet when care moves from the privacy of the home to the public market place, it ceases to be women's work and becomes the work of a certain type of woman—the immigrant woman of color.[32] It is as if society is saying that immigrant women of color have the natural propensity to do the dirty work that "normal" women will not do. Thus when Evelyn Nakano-Glenn wrote that "caring is devalued, invisible, underpaid, and penalized … relegated to those who lack economic, political, and social power and status,"[33] she hit on what until then had been a less acknowledged truth of Americans perceptions of and attitudes toward paid domestic work. Similarly, attorney and labor activist Nancy Zarate Byrd notes that women who do domestic work in the US were poor in their countries of origin and continue to be so in the US.[34] Even international bodies such as The Human Rights Watch, Amnesty International, and International Labor Organization have drawn similar conclusions about domestic care work. Taken together, these descriptions suggest a correlation between immigrant women and the work they do.[35]

These views of domestic care work call forth an analysis that re-examines some of the operational words against the diversity of paid care work in the market. There can be no doubt that caregivers' experience of work away from public view leads to isolation and invisibility but do isolation and invisibility necessarily lead to abuse and exploitation in *all types* of domestic care work? When we say that domestic work is devalued, for example, whose perspective are we representing? On what basis can we claim that immigrant domestic workers were poor in their countries of origin when some pay thousands of dollars to enter the US? These are important questions that can best be understood when analyzed from a transnational perspective that links women's lives in their countries of origin to their experiences in the new.[36]

On the matter of diversity in care work, we should note some of the differences in order to understand the Ghanaian women's work later in the book. There is care work that involves one adult caregiver and one adult care recipient where the caregiver may live in or out; other care work involves domestic arrangements where a worker lives in a household of multiple family members and performs most, if not all, of the domestic chores. There are also nannies who may or may not live with the care receiving family; and then there are care workers who work in assisted living facilities where the residents may be old, sick, or disabled. Some care workers arrive in the US with special visas to work for a particular individual or family, others enter on their own and then work with employment agencies that recruit workers for the domestic work sector, while still others, like the Ghanaian women of this study, seek out their own employment as caregivers after they have arrived in the US. Acknowledging these differences matter because it helps to avoid a "one size fits all" description of care work that can mask the diversity of experiences and perspectives within the sector.

Against this backdrop of generally delineating the link between globalization and immigration and women's location within these processes, we turn to Ghana, the country of birth of the women of this book, to analyze the interaction between globalization and the local political economy and its impact on women.

NOTES

1. This discussion is restricted to migration that was motivated by economic considerations, although I am aware that economic factors are not the only force driving the migration of people.

2. P. Rudy Mattei, "Economic I: Pull Factors," *Encyclopedia of American Immigration* (2001): 257–264; Saskia Sassen, "Economics II: Push Factors," *Encyclopedia of American Immigration* (2001): 265–278.

3. Olivier Laurent, "Haiti Earthquake: Five Years After," Time, January 2, 2015, http://time.com/3662225/haiti-earthquake-five-year-after.

4. Monica Boyd and Elizabeth Grieco, "Women and Migration: Incorporating Gender into International Migration Theory," Migration Policy Institute, March 1, 2003, http://www.migrationpolicy.org/article/women-and-migration-incorporating-gender-international-migration-theory; Aderanti Adepoju, "The Demographic Profile: Sustained High Mortality, Fertility and Migration for Employment," in Christine Oppong and Aderanti Adepoju, eds., *Gender, Work and Population in sub-Saharan Africa* (London: James Currie Ltd, 1994), 30–1; Joseph Gugler and Gudrun Ludwar-Ene, "Gender and Migration in Africa South of the Sahara," in *The Migration Experience in Africa*, ed. Jonathan Baker and Tade Akin Aina (Upsala: Nordiska Afrikainstitutet, 1995), 257.

5. Lynne Brydon, "Ghanaian Women in the Migration Process," in *Gender and Migration in Developing Countries*, ed. Sylvia Chant (London and New York: Belhaven Press, 1992); Boyd, "Women and Migration," 2003; Barbara Ehrenreich and Arlie Russell Hochschild, "Introduction," *Global Woman: Nannies, Maids and Sex Workers in the New Economy* (New York: Holt Paperbacks, 2002), 5; Priya Deshingkar and Benjamin Zeitlyn, "South-South Migration for Domestic Work and Poverty," *Geography Compass* 9, no. 4 (2015): 171.

6. Barbara Ehrenreich and Arlie Russell Hochschild, eds., *Global Woman: Nannies, Maids and Sex Workers in the New Economy* (New York: Holt Paperbacks, 2002); Eva Feder Kittay, "The Global Heart Transplant and Caring across National Boundaries," *The Southern Journal of Philosophy* 46, (2008): 138–165; Alison Weir, "Global Care Chains: Freedom, Responsibility, and Solidarity," *The Southern Journal of Philosophy* 46, (2008): 166–175; Pura Velasco, "Migrant workers amidst Globalization," in *Women in a Globalizing World: Transforming Equality, Development, Diversity and Peace*, ed. Angela Miles (Toronto: Inanna Publications and Education Inc., 2013), 284–291; Rhacel Salazar Parreñas, "Servants of Globalization: Women, Migration and Domestic Work: Migrant Filipina Domestic Workers in Role and Los Angeles," in *Feminist Theory Reader: Local and Global Perspectives*, ed. Carole R. McCann and Seung-kyun Kim, (New York: Routledge, 2013), 202–217.

7. Pat Armstrong and Hugh Armstrong, "Thinking Globally: women, Work and Caring," in *Women in a Globalizing World: Transforming Equality, Development, Diversity and Peace*, ed. Angela Miles (Toronto: Inanna Publications and Education Inc., 2013), 82.

8. Allan Brian Ssenyonga, "Americanization or Globalization," in *Taking Sides: Clashing Views on Global Issues,* ed. James E Harf and Michael O. Lombardi (New York: McGraw-Hill, 2010), 274–8.

9. Breny Mendoza, "Transnational Feminism in Question," *Feminist Theory* 3, no. 3 (2002): 316

10. David Held and Paul Hirst, "Globalization: The Argument of Our Time," Open Democracy, 2002, http://www.opendemocracy.com.

11. Rainer Tetzlaff, "World Cultures under the Pressure of Globalization: Experiences and Responses from the Different Continents," 2000, http://www.hamburgerbll-dungsserver.de/global/allgemein/tetzlaff-120.htm.

12. Martha Donkor, "Marching to the Tune: Colonization, Globalization, Immigration and the Ghanaian Diaspora," *Africa Today* 52, no.1 (Fall 2005): 28.

13. Mendoza, "Transnational Feminism," 317.

14. James C. W. Ahiakpor, "Multinational Corporations in the Third World: Predators or Allies in Economic Development? *Religion and Liberty* 2, no. 5 (September and October 1992), http://www.acton.org/pub/religion-liberty/volume-2-number-5/multinational-corporations-third-world-predators-o; Robyn Meredith and Suzanne Hoppough, "Why Globalization is Good," reprinted in *Taking Sides: Clashing Views on Global Issues,* ed. James E Harf and Michael O. Lombardi (New York: McGraw-Hill, 2010), 259–62.

15. See, for instance, Ray Kiely, "Poverty Reduction through Liberalisation? Neoliberalism and the Myth of Global Convergence," *Review of International Studies* 33, no. 3 (2007): 415–435

16. See Vikas Bajaj, "Fatal Fire in Bangladesh Highlights the Dangers Facing Garment Workers," *New York Times*, November 25, 2012, http://www.nytimes.com/2012/11/26/world/asia/bangladesh-fire-kills-more-than-100-and-injures-many.html?_r=0.

17. Donkor, "Marching to the Tune," 27.

18. Kwadwo Konadu-Agyemang, "The Best of Times and the Worst of Times: Structural Adjustment Programs and Uneven Development in Africa: The Case of Ghana," *Professional Geographer* 52, no. 3 (2000): 480–1.

19. Donkor, "Marching to the Tune," 29–30.

20. Konadu-Agyemang, "The Best of Times," 470.

21. Jana Everett and Sue Ellen M. Charlton, *Women Navigating Globalization: Feminist Approaches to Development (*Lanham: Rowman and Littlefield, 2014), 62–3.

22. Konadu-Agyemang, "The Best of Times," 473.

23. United Nations Development Program, Resource Guide: Mainstreaming Gender and Water, 2006, http://www.un.org/waterforlifedecade/gender.shtml; V. Spike Peterson and Anne Sisson Runyan, *Global Gender Issues in the New Millennium* (Boulder, CO: Westview Press, 2010), 220.

24. Hege Knutsen, "Globalisation and the Garment Industry in Sri Lanka," *Journal of Contemporary Asia* 33, no. 2 (2003): 225–250.

25. Vandana Shiva, "Our Violent Economy is hurting Women," in *Women in a Globalizing World: Transforming Equality, Development, Diversity and Peace,* ed. Angela Miles (Toronto: Inanna Publications and Education Inc., 2013), 250–251.

26. Arlie Russell Hochschild, *The Second Shift: Working Families and the Revolution at Home* (New York: Penguin Books, 2009).

27. Arlie Russell Hochschild, *The Time Bind: When Work becomes Home and Home becomes Work* (New York: Holt Paperbacks, 1997); see also Margaret Anderson and Dana Hysock: *Thinking about Women: Sociological Perspectives on Sex and Gender* (Boston: Allyn and Bacon, 2009).

28. Joya Misra, Jennifer Hickes Lundquist and Abby Templer, "Gender, Work Time, and Care Responsibilities among Faculty," *Sociological Forum* 27, no. 2 (June 2012): 308–9.

29. Anne Marie Slaughter, "Why Women Still Can't have it All," *Atlantic Monthly,* July/August, 2012, https://www.theatlantic.com/magazine/archive/2012/07/why-women-still-cant-have-it-all/309020/.

30. Arlie Hochschild, "Global Care Chains and Emotional Surplus Value," in *On the Edge: Living with Global Capitalism*, ed. Anthony Giddens and Will Hutton (London: Vintage Press, 2001), 130–46;

31. Shirlena Huang, Brenda S. A. Yeoh and Mika Toyota, "Caring for the Elderly: The Embodied Labour of Migrant Care Workers in Singapore," *Global Networks* 12, no. 2 (2012): 198–9.

32. Huang, Yeoh and Toyota, "Caring for the Elderly," 198.

33. Evelyn Nakano-Glenn, "Creating a Caring Society," *Contemporary Sociology* 29, no. 1 (Jan 2000): 84; see also Huang, Yeoh and Toyota, *Global Networks* 12, no. 2 (2012): 198.

34. Nancy Zarate Byrd, "The Dirty Side of Domestic Work: An Underground economy and the Exploitation of Undocumented Workers," *DePaul Journal for Social Justice* 3, no. 2 (Spring 2010): 246.

35. Huang, Yeoh and Totoya, "Caring for the Elderly," 199.

36. Allison Weir, "Global Care Chains: Freedom, Responsibility, and Solidarity," *The Southern Journal of Philosophy* 46, (2008): 170.

Chapter 2

Ghana in the Global Political Economy

Monday, June 4, 1979. Ghanaians awoke to the sound of military music on the airwaves. There had been a coup d'état, a violent overthrow of the government that also came to power through a coup. The leader of this latest coup was a thirty-one-year-old flight lieutenant of the Ghana armed forces, called Flt Lt J.J. Rawlings. Perhaps as a result of his age, charisma, and/or message, Rawlings became an instant sensation. Seizing on the public mood, he declared a house-cleaning exercise to weed out corruption and malfeasance in high places. That coup, and a second one he staged two years and three months later, led to the disappearance of hundreds and the murder of hundreds more, while the majority of the population cowered in fear as soldiers terrorized and students in tertiary institutions cheered them on. That violent epoch in the nation's history intensified a new kind of international migration that had begun early in the 1970s. Women actively participated in this wave of migration, the result of their being among groups of people that suffered some of the worst excesses of Rawlings' interventions in the government.

To begin, one must ask how Ghana, the first sub-Saharan African country to achieve political independence,[1] found itself in the throes of a military orchestrated "revolution" defined in terms of economic malfeasance. How had Ghana's economy performed? Was military intervention in the government a useful step in fixing a struggling economy? What roles had women played in the political and economic institutions of the country leading up to the Rawlings' coups to make them targets of revolutionary violence? These are important questions that must be critically examined to understand not only women's decisions to migrate abroad but also the tenuous relationship Ghana's economy has had with global economic forces.

Centuries before globalization became a buzzword, Ghana was participating in global trade. Ruins of forts as well as castles in active use that

Europeans built along the coast as trading posts stand as testament to Ghana's early participation in global trade. From Keta in the east to Dixcove in the west, the nearly 350-mile coastline held thirty-two forts and castles, the largest concentration of European trading posts in sub-Saharan Africa. The first Europeans to arrive in Ghana were the Portuguese in the 1470s, nearly two decades before Christopher Columbus reached the western hemisphere. By 1485, the Portuguese had completed building a castle at Elmina (corrupted form of La Mina, Portuguese for "the mine").[2] The Portuguese' choice of Elmina as the site to build a trading post was telling. There was a brisk trade already going on among the coastal peoples and those from the forest region in the hinterland when the Portuguese arrived. The people along the coast and those from the hinterland traded in gold, salt, fish, etc. Early observers say that gold was exchanged for its weight in salt.[3] The hinterland was rich in gold but there were no salt deposits. The coastal people had salt that they mined from the lagoons in the coastal marshes but they did not have the quantities of gold that the people in the forest region had. The only way that the people who inhabited the forest areas could obtain salt was to trek miles to the coast; and while at the coast, they exchanged gold and other forest produce for salt and fish. This trade among the peoples of Ghana went on for a considerable length of time. I remember my grandfather used to tell us stories around the fire at night about how his great-great-grandfather was reputed to have put a grain of salt in his mouth and then eat his food instead of putting salt in the food for the entire family. That was how valuable salt was in the hinterland, and those who had it guarded it jealously. It was this trade that the Portuguese and then other Europeans including the British and Dutch exploited and developed into a global trade in ways that the early local traders could not have imagined. It was this trade in salt, gold, fish, etc., that developed into principally a trade in slaves that lasted into the nineteenth century and then reverted to what the Europeans called legitimate trade when the transatlantic slave trade was abolished in 1808.[4]

By the time Europeans partitioned Africa in 1884 and declared official spheres of influence, Ghana had had contact with the Western world through trade for about 400 years. Families, chiefdoms and kingdoms flourished as they participated in coastal, ergo, international trade. This should not be construed to mean that European presence was beneficial to the peoples of Ghana.[5] Chiefs, kings, and their families benefited at the expense of their own people. The change in status of the various communities along the coast—from independent chiefdoms to a colonized state (called Gold Coast) in 1874 by the British—changed Ghana's relationship with the global economy. Instead of trading and profiting from trade directly as individuals or representatives of powerful chiefdoms, the local people found themselves marginalized in the conduct of international trade. No longer were they able to determine whom they would trade with and on what terms; those decisions were made by the British, who were the colonial masters. Thus began Ghana's tenuous relationship with the global political economy. Africanist historians have long grappled with the meaning and impact of European contact and colonization on Africans. Two of these scholars offer opposing viewpoints that merit mention here. In *How Europe Underdeveloped Africa*, Walter Rodney states that the European colonial enterprise was fashioned specifically and intentionally to impoverish Africa. The colonial enterprise was exploitative and dehumanizing, siphoning resources from colonized sites while leaving the colonized countries impoverished and dependent.[6] On the other hand, Basil Davidson argues that Africans' relationship with the global economy within the context of colonization was complex and contradictory, with a gain in one area offset by a larger "net loss."[7] Davidson demonstrates, for example, that the introduction of banks, shipping lines, and wholesale businesses by the colonial masters modernized African economies; however, Africans did not reap direct benefits from these ventures, if they did at all. In the agricultural sector, individual farmers who produced export crops such as cocoa, coffee, and groundnuts could sell their products and make a profit, although, again, the farmers did not have any control over the pricing of their produce.[8]

In the case of Ghana, mining, lumbering, and cocoa production became important avenues for people to participate in global trade. Since mining and lumbering were and are still male-typed occupations, we can assume that women did not directly participate in those activities. And although we do not have records of women's participation in international trade at that point, it is possible that they benefited as mothers, wives, daughters, and nieces of men who engaged in the production of export commodities. What is significant about the export market is what Frimpong-Ansah has described as an economic dependency syndrome necessitated by production and consumption patterns. The peoples of Ghana, like other colonized Africans, were encouraged to produce for export goods they did not eat but which the British needed to keep their industrial complexes running, and to consume what they did not produce.[9] Ghana did not have manufacturing plants that would use its raw materials; however, the production of raw materials generated wealth with which the elite could purchase and consume foreign manufactured goods. The upshot has been a dependency relationship of Ghana with the West that endures to this day.

In terms of political development, the partitioning and colonization of Ghana changed the relations that the peoples had with the British. Until the partitioning, the various groups were autonomous entities, sometimes fighting with each other for supremacy and control of resources, including coastal trade.[10] Europeans trading along the coast were restricted to coastal towns and dabbled in local politics at their own peril.[11] The partitioning and eventual takeover of the coastal regions of Ghana changed the relations among the peoples on the one hand, and then the peoples and the British, on the other. The various communities were bundled together into a new political entity and given a new name, the Gold Coast. But Ghana had one advantage going for it. It was not a settler colony but a protectorate; as such there was relatively limited presence of British colonial officials when compared with settler colonies like Kenya. And unlike places like Nigeria and Kenya where the British created the office of the chief as the liaison between them and the local people, the British in Ghana used traditional chieftaincy institutions that were already firmly established and functioning. Unfortunately, the British ignored female political office holders and dealt mainly with men instead, perhaps a reflection of their patriarchal tendencies that led them to marginalize their own women in the political processes in Britain.

The system of Indirect Rule, the British framework of colonial administration in West Africa, served the colonizers well to the extent that the local chiefs held their subjects in check and the chiefs themselves did not rebel against colonial authority.[12] Any show of insubordination was dealt with harshly. For example, in March 1900, an Asante queen mother called Yaa Asantewaa defied the British governor's demand for a sacred royal object for his personal use. Yaa Asantewaa first verbally attacked the male chiefs for cowering in the presence of the British governor, and then vowed to fight if the governor insisted on his demand. Her open challenge to British authority led to a war between the two sides with the British descending on the Asante with the full force of empire.[13] Troops from Nigeria and Sierra Leone were brought in to quell what the British described as a rebellion. By November 1900 the Asante had been defeated, the queen mother and other chiefs were captured and exiled to the Seychelles Islands in the Indian Ocean north of Madagascar. The way was then cleared for the British to expand their jurisdiction beyond the coastal areas into the gold-rich hinterland that Asante controlled until its defeat. The British response to the Asante, it seems to me, was not simply that the Asante flouted their authority; it appears that the British did not like that a woman led that charge.

The foregoing brief historical analysis gives an insight into economic and political developments in Ghana before it attained independence in 1957. Ghana's independence was remarkable for being the first sub-Saharan African country to attain independence. But even as Ghana basked in the glory of its political achievement, calling itself the "Black Star of Africa," its political and economic condition was slowly unraveling. The country was not showing much economic promise or political maturity. It could neither significantly expand nor diversify the economic system established during the colonial period. In terms of the economic conditions, several observers indicate that the seeds of economic decline were sown before the decade of the 1960s ended.[14] Frimpong-Ansah's assessment of the state of Ghana's economy after 1966 reveals the depths into which the country had fallen. He notes that "[Nkrumah] left behind a legacy of economic decline, with a fragile external sector, heavy debts, a delicate fiscal structure, an export sector in which the seeds of destruction had been sown ... [and] an impoverished urban class that was to haunt all successor governments."[15]

By the early 1970s Ghana was caught in the throes of a cycle of high inflation, poverty, low levels of food production and unprecedented levels of corruption, the latter expressed in a new slang called "kalabule."[16] Consumer goods like sugar, milk, flour, and rice were in short supply; the cedi, the unit of the currency, depreciated in value; and the general feeling was that life was hard.

The political situation was equally volatile. The leaders of Ghana could not adapt political structures that would reflect new political realities. Independence put Ghanaians in absolute control of governance but the process was so mismanaged that military interventions became a recurring feature in Ghana's political culture until 1992. Indeed, between 1966 and 1982 there were six governments but only two were constitutionally elected civilian governments. The remaining four were military regimes established as a result of coup d'état. I would surmise that military interventions in government reflected a case of individual ambition for aggrandizement and not a deep-seated understanding of the complexity of governance and the ability of the military strong men to work to reform the system. None of the military governments substantially improved the economic conditions in the country for which they forcefully took over power. Deborah Pellow and Naomi Chazan have observed that the military governments were inept and authoritarian, and together caused social, political, and economic decline.[17] For instance, in January 1972, a democratically elected government was ousted by the military on the grounds of economic hardship. The ensuing military regime, euphemistically named National Redemption Council, could not redeem the country from economic decline. That regime was reconstituted and renamed Supreme Military Council (SMC) in 1975 only to be taken over in a bloodless house coup in 1978 and renamed SMC II. SMC II had been in office a month shy of its first anniversary when the coup on Monday, June 4, 1979, occurred.[18]

While people do not wake up expecting a violent military takeover of government, it is doubtful whether Ghanaians were overly surprised to hear that there had been yet another coup that Monday morning. After all, there had been a failed attempt only a month earlier and Rawlings, the leader, had been tried and sentenced. He was in prison when some junior officers staged the June 4 coup, released him from prison, and declared him the leader of the coup. News of the coup was thus received with mixed feelings. Some people hoped that the new leaders would arrest the downward economic spiral while others viewed the situation as one of those military takeovers that did nothing to bring about any positive changes to society. But it soon became apparent that this coup was unlike any of the previous ones. Rawlings had a message and persona that resonated with the people, especially university students. He identified himself as a poor person, as one of the people and railed against corrupt politicians, traders, and others who he accused of ruining the country. He joined university students to cart cocoa beans from inaccessible rural areas to urban centers, joined citizens to clean dirty streets and gutters, and reminded people of their power and ownership of the country. He adopted a populist strategy by claiming that ordinary Ghanaians had been taken advantage of by unscrupulous politicians and traders. With the singular ambition of cleaning house, that is, freeing society from corruption and giving power to the people, Rawlings' populist message resonated with a large segment of the Ghanaian population—students, underemployed, and unemployed urban poor. "Power to the people," "we no go sit down make them cheat us every day," and other revolutionary slogans and songs were carefully crafted and widely circulated on the airwaves several times a day to give a sense of euphoria to the downtrodden people in Ghanaian society.[19]

Depending on perspective, one could say that it was an exciting or uncertain time in Ghana's history. People who believed that the new regime was going to transform the country were excited about the new prospects, while others viewed with skepticism the lawlessness that was unfolding. Rawlings created the Armed Forces Revolutionary Council as the government of the country and suspended the constitution. He (affectionately called "Junior Jesus" by his supporters because of his initials J.J.) became head of state. With soldiers patrolling the streets to enforce a six p.m. to six a.m. curfew nationwide, there was fear but also the promise of profound transformation of social, economic, and political life. There was no nightlife in the country for several weeks after the coup. Businesses that operated at night such as restaurants and nightclubs, and women who sold cooked food along the streets suffered greatly. Daytime trading also became a very risky business as citizens could rush in, buy goods, and then determine how much they thought the goods were worth and paid that price. In the meantime, politicians, entrepreneurs, and big traders were coming under intense attacks. Private investments and businesses were confiscated and transferred to state ownership; some high-ranking military officers, including two former military heads of state, were tried in hastily constituted military tribunals for an assortment of alleged crimes against the state, found guilty and executed. People disappeared, never to be seen or heard from again.[20]

Market women were particularly vulnerable. They were believed to have created artificial shortages by hoarding goods. They were targeted and brutalized. In the two largest cities, Accra and Kumasi, and other urban centers, market women could be arrested, stripped naked, and publicly flogged. Sometimes they were made to squat while naked, hold their ears, and then hop around as they recite, "I'm stubborn, I won't do that again" while being lashed at the back.[21] The central market in Accra, which had been the hub for most female traders, was bulldozed to stop women's trading activities.[22] Further north, at the largest outdoor market in the country at Techiman, soldiers and police officers patrolled and monitored and often beat traders. Even in small towns and villages, petty traders came under intense scrutiny and attack from militias. Those who refused to sell their wares out of fear were accused of hoarding; those who ignored the warning signs and sold their goods were also accused of selling above the "controlled" prices. Traders just could not win. Many lost their capital and a few lost their lives through the violence. Some traders in urban areas rejoined their families in the rural areas where military brutality was not as severe while others stayed on hoping for good times.[23]

This entire house-cleaning exercise lasted for three months. Elections were held later in 1979 and the country returned to civilian rule. By all accounts, Ghana had passed through fire, but was it purged? The country's return to civilian rule in late 1979 was supposed to signal a new era. Stores gradually filled with goods, traders were not afraid to do business, and even kalabule resurfaced. Politics gave people something to talk about, and by all indications, life was returning to normal, even if in measured steps. Then in the early hours of December 31, 1981, the news of yet another coup was broadcast. Rawlings was back, this time declaring a "holy war" against corruption. He suspended the constitution as before, dissolved parliament and established the Provisional National Defence Council (PNDC) as the governing body of the country and again declared himself the leader. All political parties were proscribed and in their place local councils composed of civilians called People's Defence Committees (PDCs) were created. In early 1984 the PDCs were renamed Committees for the Defence of the Revolution (CDRs), a clear break with the populist agenda of the previous years to one geared toward safeguarding the political machinery Rawlings had created. As with the previous coup, politicians and professionals who opposed the policies and methods of the new regime, business people who were believed to have caused economic problems, and people who were suspected of being hostile to the regime were all targeted as "enemies of the revolution" and harassed. Executions, disappearances, and imprisonment without trial, confiscation and appropriation of property became the order of the day.[24]

In spite of the economic hardship that the revolution caused, government decreed in 1982 that individuals having more than two hundred cedis in fifty cedi notes must deposit their money at the bank. Whether or not this was a smart economic move to reduce money in circulation in order to arrest inflation is difficult to determine; it is also hard to tell whether the directive was a ploy to take money from the people to run the country instead of borrowing from external sources. Whatever the government's motive, the exercise further distressed traders, especially small traders with limited capital, majority of who were women. People in rural areas where there were no banking facilities found themselves in a quandary regarding the directive to take fifty-cedi notes to the bank. In towns where there were banking facilities, long lines formed as people tried to deposit their money. I recall a cocoa farmer in my village who put his fifty-cedi notes in a large sack and set it on fire instead of traveling to the city only twelve miles away to deposit the money at the bank. Others were not as dramatic; they simply left their money to go waste. Unfortunately for such people, the rains failed during the farming season in 1983. The drought led to bush fires that destroyed both cash and food crops. The food situation was so dire that the international donor community had to step in to save Ghana from total collapse. [25] Indeed, an analyst of Ghana's political economy commented in 1983 that "to some extent, Ghana [was] a state only because the outside world assert[ed] that there was a Ghanaian state."[26] Small traders like my mother who relied on farmers for produce to sell saw their businesses collapse. My mother, for example, was not able to revive her produce selling business after 1983. She has since been doing subsistence agriculture, something she previously did during the lean season when crops for sale were not yet in yield. One can assume that my mother was lucky. At least she could go back to farming when the rains returned. Other women were not as lucky.

ENTER THE IMF AND WORLD BANK

Against the very harsh political and economic realities, the PNDC government did something that would have been unthinkable in the first year of its so-called revolution. In 1983, Rawlings, who had initially railed against the West because of its sins of "neos"—neoliberalism, neocolonialism, and neoimperialism—that he claimed had destroyed independent African countries, turned to the World Bank and IMF for assistance to arrest the economic decline. [27] That move was a stark indication that the decrees, executions, confiscations, and public floggings had not succeeded in fixing the economy. In fact, there was more hardship than when the revolution began. And like everywhere else that the World Bank and IMF have given loans, Ghana could obtain loans within the framework of SAPs, called Economic Recovery Program in Ghana. SAPs were code for the recipient country to abandon its old ways of managing its economy to one dictated by the lending institutions modeled on Western economies.[28] In the case of Ghana, the conditions the lending institutions spelled out included devaluation of the currency, downsizing the workforce, drastic budget cuts, and the withdrawal of government subsidies to state-owned institutions.[29] SAPs became another layer of austerity imposed on an already fragile economy and people who were economically stressed. The introduction of SAPs had an immediate and negative effect. Inflation spiraled out of control; unemployment soared and created hardship for families; traders who were on their way to recovery saw their businesses shrink again. Importers found their businesses come to a standstill when government outlawed the use of foreign currency by private individuals. Yet, the international donor community hailed Ghana as a country on the path to recovery, modernization, and development because it had embarked on structural adjustment. Rawlings received legitimacy, and dissenters and protesters of his policies were hounded and ran out of town without condemnation from the international community.

By the mid-1980s the worst excesses of the revolution had died down, but Ghana continued to be run as a military dictatorship. One can only say that the resilience of the people won the day. Goods reappeared on the market, rumors of attempted coups died down, and the semblance of a free media began to emerge. With pressure from the international community, Rawlings decided to return the country to civilian rule in the late 1980s.[30] He had been a military dictator for nine years. But it appeared he was not yet ready to leave the political scene. He formed a political party, the National Democratic Congress (NDC), with a slogan of "probity and accountability." In 1992, for the first time in thirteen years, Ghanaians went to the polls. Rawlings' party won an election that the main opposition party described as stolen. The man who burst onto the political scene as a fiery military revolutionary had now morphed into a democratically elected civilian president. He would serve two four-year terms, making him the person with the longest record of ruling Ghana since it attained independence. He ruled Ghana for nineteen years.

Women in the Ghanaian Political Economy

In all the twists and turns in the economic and political evolution of Ghana, women did not occupy center stage, although it is possible that they played important roles. The dearth of information on women during the colonial period makes it difficult to reconstruct a complete account of their activities. Nonetheless, there is research that shows that some women engaged in high-level business ventures while others performed important political duties on behalf of their people. McCaskie, eminent historian of Ghana, states that one Amma Sika and her husband obtained a mining concession from an Asante chief in 1895.[31] Akurang-Parry also examines the activism of elite women and details the numerous ways in which such women made their presence felt in the Gold Coast.[32] Similarly, Trevor Getz uses the case of one woman to show the application of colonial law toward bonded women who tried to use the legal system to secure their freedom,[33] while Beatrix Allah-Mensah analyzes women's roles in the nationalist movement that ushered Ghana to independence.[34] From these studies we get a picture, albeit incomplete, of women's lives during the colonial period. They might not have made major economic and political decisions, but like women elsewhere who lived under patriarchal systems, a small minority had the opportunity to make their presence felt in society.

The post-independence period opened with a flurry of research on African women generally and Ghanaian women in particular. Ester Boserup spearheaded research on African women with her 1970 study on African women's economic activities. A major highlight of her study was that African women were overburdened with layers of labor at home and in the fields as agricultural laborers.[35] Subsequent critique of that literature reveals that Boserup's frame of reference was the West, thus stripping African women of the cultural contexts in which they participated in economic activities.[36] Ghanaian women, like women elsewhere in Africa, engaged in economic activities based on the traditions that governed the lives of people in different ethnic groups. Among the matrilineal Akan, for example, Gwendolyn Mikell showed that women could own land that they could develop on their own behalf. Unfortunately, many were unable to cultivate large cash crop plantations because, as wives, they worked on their husbands' plantations in addition to cultivating food crops for the family; as such they did not have enough time to cultivate large "own account" cocoa farms.[37] But that did not mean that Akan women did not have access to cash. They might not have cultivated cocoa, a major export crop, to the same degree as men, but they cultivated vegetables—pepper, groundnuts, garden eggs, okra—and other foodstuff for the local market. Similarly Lynne Brydon's study of the patrilineal Ewe of Avatime revealed that women were not allowed to cultivate rice, the chief food crop of that people, due to tradition.[38] If rice were an export crop, the women would not have reaped any profits since they would have been barred from its production. Along the coast where the land could not support large-scale crop production, women engaged in different kinds of economic activities depending on the resources in their local communities. Women whose family members were fishermen worked closely with the men. They sold the catch, fresh or smoked. Women who were not involved in the fish trade could sell cooked food or imported wares at the markets dotting the towns and villages along the coast. Wolf Bleek has noted that Ghanaian women participated in the economy from the margins largely because of their lack of formal education.[39]

As incomes rose among economically active people, a new expression—the play man—emerged among the Akan that described the petty bourgeois of society. Although the expression is gender specific, its application is gender neutral. It was and still is used to apply to women by merely tagging "woman" on as in "play man woman." The play man woman described a confident, self-made woman, married or not, who ran her own business, owned some property, and/or somehow exhibited confidence, independence, and a flair for fashion. Interestingly, educated women were not called "play man" women. Educated women had their own title.

Ghanaian women were economically active and did not restrict themselves to a single money-making enterprise. Many engaged in multiple economic activities concurrently. For example, a female teacher may supplement her income by selling lingerie, bedsheets, and shoes. But it was as market women that women dominated the retail trade. The "market woman" emerged as an economic institution. Although women dominated the retail trade, there were gender differences in the kinds of goods they traded in and the size of their businesses. Women dominated the sale of perishable food items and non-heavy duty manufactured goods such as fabrics, hygiene products, and kitchenware. Given the nature of their trade goods and size of their businesses, it is safe to assume that female traders did not own large initial capital, although it is also likely that they had small cash on hand all the time because of quick turnover. Market women wielded and continue to wield considerable social, economic, and political power, part of the reason they became targets for harassment during the turbulent years of Rawlings' revolution. Some were play man women, ergo, independent women who were probably seen as a threat to the patriarchy.

In politics, women's participation, as in other parts of Africa, has been the subject of interesting interpretations. Jean O'Barr and Kathryn Fimin-Sellers, for instance, state that before European colonization, African women exercised political power in varying degrees in different societies; however, European contact changed that dynamic and saw African women marginalized politically.[40] That mode of analysis, while useful in delineating the gendered dimensions of European colonization in Africa, does not adequately capture the diverse character of political systems that the Europeans established to deal with the equally diverse political institutions Africans already had in place. The lack of attention to diversity that Boserup championed in the analysis of African women's economic experiences was transferred to analysis of other realms of African women's social and political life. The result has been historical analyses about African women that cast them as victims with very little or no political agency. That portrayal cannot be entirely accurate, certainly in Ghana, when set against the type of colony and the reach of British influence.

In Ghana the British were not able to penetrate and culturally influence the interior until after 1900 when they defeated and colonized the Asante kingdom and temporarily abolished the Asante monarchy (which they restored in 1935).[41] Other areas in the interior did not lose their traditional political structures or functions due to the abolition of the Asante monarchy. Queen mothers in these areas continued to exercise their power within the realm of traditional political authority in regard to their people. Women lost out in political importance when colonial officials dealt directly with traditional authority. For instance, in 1927 the British passed the Native Administrative Ordinance that gave Native Tribunals the right to try witchcraft cases. The tribunals did not include queen mothers.[42] Thus, O'Barr and Fimin-Sellers were right to indicate that women were marginalized politically, but that is only to a certain extent. Queen mothers in the interior of Ghana, for example, continued to exercise their social and spiritual authority (which had been their major roles, anyway) in their respective cultural contexts.[43] Ultimately, in the post-independence era, a two-tiered political system evolved: it is made up of civil society, where affairs of state are handled, and traditional society, where matters pertaining to specific ethnic groups as defined by their ethnic lore and customs are observed. This hybridized form of political structure seems to serve the needs of the people well. Government recognizes the authority of chiefs and queen mothers as guardians of land and culture. There is, in fact, a national house of chiefs and a corresponding national house of queen mothers. These institutions not only are revered nationally but also sway public opinion on important national issues.

It is important to note that the period leading to independence ushered in an avenue for women to step onto the public political stage. No longer did women have to rely on blood in their families (as queen mothers) to be able to exercise political power. They joined the nationalist movement that gave Ghana independence and then joined newly formed political parties and established women's wings to mobilize women to the parties' causes.[44] The twenty-first century has ushered in a new era for women's political participation. Politicians must be democratically elected based on popular appeal and message. Women have risen to the occasion, albeit at a slower pace than one might desire. Leaders of women's wings of political parties wield immense power; unfortunately, their roles as party activists have not always translated into positions in national political office. Table 2.1 shows women who were elected to Parliament for selected administrations from the first republic in 1960 until the 7th parliament of the 4th republic in 2017.

As can be seen from the table, there were ten women in the parliament of the first Republic in 1960. What happened with these elected female parliamentarians was that the government organized special elections in order to

Table 2.1 Representation of Women in Selected Parliaments, 1960–2017

Year	*1960*	*1969*	*1979*	*1992*	*1996*	*2000*	*2004*	*2017*
Gov't	1st Rep.	2nd Rep.	3rd Rep.	4th Rep.	2nd Par.	3rd Par.	4th Par.	7th Par.
Seats	104	140	140	200	200	200	230	275
Women	10	2	5	6	18	19	25	36
Men	94	138	135	194	182	181	205	239
% Women	9.6	1.4	3.6	3	9	9.5	10.9	13.1

Notes: Allah-Mensah, *Women in Politics*, 28; Government of Ghana, http://www.parliament.gh/mps?az&P=14; Pathways of Women's Empowerment, February 11, 2008, http://pathwaysghana.blogspot.com/2008/02/womens-participation-in-politics-in.html.
Source: After every military regime a new republic is proclaimed. The 4th republic came into being in 1993; each election cycle ushers in a new parliament. Rep. is short for Republic; Par. is short for Parliament.

have women represented in government; otherwise there would have been none.[45] Subsequent governments did not build on this affirmative action initiative, although the various parties that have since contested elections have had strong women's wings with qualified women who could fill important positions.

The PNDC, in spite of its military rhetoric and initial atrocities, should be credited with giving women avenues to wield public political power. Although only six women were elected to parliament nationwide in 1992 during the first civilian administration of Rawlings, women held important political positions. The most prominent female member of the Rawlings' political machine (although she did not hold an appointed or elected office other than being first lady) was Mrs. Konadu-Agyemang-Rawlings. She worked closely with her husband to steer the PNDC throughout its existence as the governing authority in Ghana. During Ghana's transition from the PNDC era to parliamentary rule, Mrs. Rawlings and her husband founded the NDC that won two presidential cycles in 1992 and 1996. That means that Mrs. Rawlings was first lady for nineteen years, from 1982 to 2000. In those years she represented Ghana at international women's forums and founded and chaired the 31st December Women's Movement to mobilize women at the grassroots. When she felt the NDC was not upholding the principles that she and her husband enunciated she left and founded her own party, the National Democratic Party.[46] Other high-profile women of the PNDC administration included Cecilia Johnson, Joyce Aryee, and Mary Grant. The NDC government continued the tradition set by the PNDC; in its tenure as the ruling party from 2012 to 2016 (5th and 6th parliaments of the 4th Republic), the NDC filled nine cabinet positions (out of a total of twenty-five) with women. Other important positions occupied by women included the Speaker of Parliament, Chief Justice, and the Electoral Commissioner. Women's prospects appear to have dipped slightly under the current New Patriotic Party (NPP) government. Only nine (out of thirty-three) cabinet positions are held by women, as illustrated in Table 2.2.

Table 2.2 Cabinet Positions held by Women, 6th and 7th Parliaments of the 4th Republic

6th Parliament (2012–2016)	*7th Parliament (2017–)*
Minister of Foreign Affairs	Minister of Foreign Affairs
Minister of Gender and Social Protection	Minister of Gender and Social Protection
Minister of Health	Attorney General and Minister of Justice
Minister of State (Presidency)	Minister of Communications
Minister of State (Presidency)	Minister of Local Government
Minister of Transport	Minister of Fisheries and Aquaculture
Attorney General	Minister of Aviation
Minister of Education	Minister of Tourism, Arts, and Culture
Employment and Labor Relation	Minister of Special Development Initiatives

Source: Parliament of Ghana, http://www.parliament.gh/mps?leadership.

Other important political positions currently held by women include the Chief of Staff, Secretary to the Cabinet, Deputy Majority Leader, Second Deputy Minority Chief Whip and Chief Justice. Eight other women have also been appointed as deputy ministers of state. Ironically, not even one woman has been named as regional minister in the 7th Parliament, and only three are serving as deputy regional ministers from the ten regions.[47] What is significant about women's cabinet portfolios is that they are not gender-typed, with the exception of the Ministries of Gender and Education.

Women's participation in politics reflects gains they have made in education since independence. During the colonial period women's education was not a priority to the colonial masters. The colonial officials relied on men as subordinates and so they focused their educational efforts on men.[48] After independence the attitude toward female education changed and government and religious bodies made efforts to increase girls' enrollment at all levels of the education system. However, traditional practices coupled with poverty have circumscribed the efforts of many women to receive an education.[49] In spite of that, educated Ghanaian women have infiltrated so-called non-traditional job areas as doctors, lawyers, politicians, professors, and law enforcement officers, albeit in relatively smaller numbers. And like women in most places, Ghanaian women dominate elementary- and secondary-level teaching, nursing, and secretarial work. In the large urban areas, women work as beauticians, restauranteurs, dressmakers, hairdressers, and storeowners. Thousands more work daily as peddlers, porters, and petty traders largely because their educational background is not sufficient to afford them entry into the formal sector.

Clearly, Ghanaian women have come a long way. Like every society, Ghana is constantly in flux and the women have responded to change in diverse ways. They grappled with the forces of colonization and globalization, and they endured revolutionary violence in which some saw their fortunes wiped out. There cannot be a single narrative that can accurately capture the experiences and status of Ghanaian women. But one thing is certain.

Women in Ghana love to trade but may not always have the capital necessary to do so. With limited resources at their disposal, some have looked to immigration as an avenue to acquire the means to achieve their goals. Whether or not they are successful in that quest remains to be seen.

NOTES

1. That distinction would have gone to Sudan, whose independence from the British was scheduled to take effect in 1956 but the process was derailed by a civil war that finally ended with the creation of South Sudan in 2011. See Martha Donkor, Sudanese Refugees in the United States: The Collateral Damage of Sudan's Civil War (Lewiston: The Edwin Mellen Press, 2008), 40.

2. Gordon Kerr, *Short History of Africa: From the Origins of Human History to the Arab Spring* (Herpenden: Oldcastle Book, 2012), 38.

3. Peter A. Schweizer, *Survivors on the Gold Coast: The Basel Missionaries in Colonial Ghana* (Accra: Smartline Publishing, 2001), 42.

4. Raymond E. Dumett, *El Dorado in West Africa: The Gold Mining Frontier, African Labor, and Colonial Capitalism in the Gold Coast, 1875–1900* (Athens, Ohio: Ohio University Press, 1998), 3.

5. The Akwamu kingdom and Asante empire were forged through conquest because of their possession of firearms which they purchased from the Europeans and active participation in the slave trade. Ultimately, leaders and their families of these political entities benefited from their expansionist agendas while many ordinary people were sold as slaves or used as soldiers, porters, and servants in the service of the kings and their councils of elders. See Trevor R. Getz and Liz Clarke, *Abina and the Important Men: A Graphic History* (New York: Oxford University Press. 2011).

6. Walter Rodney, *How Europe Underdeveloped Africa* (London: Bogle-L'Ouverture Publications, 1972).

7. Basil Davidson, *Modern Africa: A Social and Political History* (Harlow: Longman, 1994), 19.

8. Davidson, *Modern Africa* 17–19.

9. Jonathan H. Frimpong-Ansah, *The Vampire State in Africa: The Political Economy of Decline in Ghana* (London: James Currie Ltd, 1991), 130.

10. Schweizer, *Survivors on the Gold Coast*, 43.

11. For instance, in 1824, the British governor of Sierra Leone, Sir Charles McCarthy, inserted himself in the enmity and wars between the Fanti along the coast and the powerful Asante in the interior of Ghana and was killed. See Funso Afolayan, "Kingdoms of West Africa: Benin, Oyo, and Asante," in *African History before 1885*, ed. Toyin Falola *Africa: African History before 1885*, vol. 1 (Durham, NC: Carolina Academic Press, 2003), 185.

12. Natasha Gray, "Witches, Oracles, and Colonial Law: Evolving Anti-Witchcraft Practices in Ghana, 1927–1932," *The International Journal of African Historical Studies* 34, no.2 (2001): 347; T.C. McCaskie, "The Life and Afterlife of Yaa Asantewaa," *Africa* 77, no. 2 (2007): 157.

13. Dumett, *El Dorado in West Africa,* 287.

14. Frimpong-Ansah, *The Vampire State in Africa*; Deborah Pellow and Naomi Chazan, *Ghana: Coping with Uncertainty* (Boulder, Colo.: Westview Press, 1986); Oppong and Abu, *Marriage among a Matrilineal Elite: Seven Roles of Women*, 18.

15. Frimpong-Ansah, *The Vampire State in Africa*, 97.

16. Pellow and Chazan, *Ghana: Coping with Uncertainty*, 58.

17. Pellow and Chazan, *Coping with Uncertainty*, 47.

18. Edward Reynolds, "Ghana, Republic of: Acheampong Regime to the Third Republic, 1972–1981," in *Encyclopedia of African History,* ed. Kevin Shillington (London: Routledge, 2004), https://voyager.ship.edu/rpas/ezproxy.cgi?institution=15&url=http://search.credoreference.com/content/entry/routafricanhistory/ghana_republic_of_acheampong_regime_to_the_third_republic_1972_1981/0?institutionId=649.

19. Nii K. Bensti-Enchill, "Shaping a Revolution," *West Africa* January 3 (1983): 5–7.

20. Kevin Shillington, *Ghana and the Rawlings Factor* (London: Macmillan, 1992); Edward Opoku-Dapaah, "Ghana 1981–1991: A Decade of Forced Repression and Migration." *Refuge* 11, no. 3, (1992): 8–13.

21. A businessman from my village who lived in the city was brought to the village and made to go through that type of punishment but he was not stripped naked, an indication of how the military meted out that kind of punishment based on gender.

22. Pellow and Chazan, *Coping with Uncertainty*, 60–62.

23. Pellow and Chazan, *Coping with Uncertainty*, 61.

24. Nii K. Bentsi-Enchill, "Shaping a Revolution," *West Africa*, January 3, 1983, 5–7; Opoku-Dapaah, "Decade of Repression," 10–11.

25. Bentsi-Enchill, "Ghana Absorbs its Own," *West Africa*, February 14, 1983, 382–385.

26. Quoted in Jeffery Herbst, *The Politics of Reform in Ghana, 1982–1992* (Berkeley: University of California Press, 1993), 14.

27. World Bank: Sector Policy Paper, 1980, 87.

28. Lindsay Whitfield, "Trustees of Development from Conditionality to Governance: Poverty Reduction Strategy Papers in Ghana," *The Journal of Modern African Studies* 43, no. 4 (Dec 2005): 643.

29. Bade Onimode, ed., *The IMF, The World Bank and the African Debt: The Economic Impact* (London and New Jersey: Zed Books, 1989), 48.

30. Kwame Boafo-Arthur, "A Decade of Liberalism in Perspective," in *Ghana: One Decade of the Liberal State*, ed., Kwame Boafo-Arthur (London: Zed Books, 2007), 2.

31. McCaskie, "Life and Afterlife of Yaa Asantewaa," 157.

32. Kwabena O. Akurang-Parry, "Aspects of Elite Women's Activism in the Gold Coast, 1874–1890," *International Journal of African Historical Studies* 37, no. 3 (2004): 463–482.

33. Trevor R. Getz and Liz Clarke, *Abina and the Important Men: A Graphic History* (New York: Oxford University Press, 2011).

34. Beatrix Allah-Mensah, *Women in Politics and Public Life in Ghana* (Accra: Friedrich-Ebert Foundation, 2005), 14.

35. Ester Boserup, *Woman's Role in Economic Development* (London: George Allen and Unwin, 1970).

36. "Problematic Aspects in Ester Boserup's *Woman's Role in Economic Development*, http://www.africaresource.com/essays-a-reviews/gender/131-problematic-aspects-of-ester-boserups-womans-role-in-economic-development?showall=&start=3; see also "Culture, Gender and Development," Report submitted to the African Institute for Economic Development and Planning by The Centre for Gender and Social Policy Studies, Obafemi Awolowo University, Ile-Ife, Nigeria, Dakar, Senegal, October 2001.

37. Gwendolyn Mikell, "Ghanaian Females, Rural Economy and National Stability," *African Studies Review* 29, no. 3 (September 1986), 74.

38. Lynne Brydon, "The Dimensions of Subordination: A Case Study from Avatime," in *Women, Work and Ideology*, ed. Haleh Afshar (London: Tavistock Publications, 1985), 114.

39. Wolf Bleek, "Family and Family Planning in Southern Ghana," in *Sex Roles, Population and Development in West Africa,* edited by Christine Oppong (London: James Currie, 1987), 147–150.

40. Jean O'Barr and Kathryn Fimin-Sellers, "African Women in Politics," in *African Women South of the Sahara*, ed. Margaret Jean Hay and Sharon Stichter, (New York: John Wiley and Sons, 1995), 89.

41. McCaskie, "Life and Afterlife of Yaa Asantewaa," 151.

42. Gray, "Witches, Oracles, and Colonial Law," 348.

43. See McCaskie, "Life and Afterlife of Yaa Asantewaa," 153–9.

44. Allah-Mensah, *Women in Politics*, 14; Abdul-Gafaru Abdulai, "Political Context Study—Ghana," Human Rights, Power and Civic Action Research Project, Universities of Oslo, Leeds and Ghana, January 2009, http://www.polis.leeds.ac.uk/assets/files/research/research-projects/abdulai-ghana-political-context-study-jan09.pdf.

45. Elsie Quaicoe-Duho, "Female MP in Ghana's First Republic shares her Experience—Calls for Peaceful Elections," Becce quaicoe's Library, December 3, 2012, 2016, http://becceq7317.blogspot.com/2012/12/female-mp-in-ghana-first-republic.html.

46. She contested for the presidency in the 2016 election although the Electoral Commissioner initially disqualified her for clerical errors in her filing documents. For more details, see www.ghanaweb.com, October 11, 2016.

47. Parliament of Ghana, accessed February 5, 2017, http://www.parliament.gh/mps?leadership.

48. Obed Mfum-Mensah, *Education, Social Progress, and Marginalized Children in Sub-Saharan Africa: Historical Antecedents and Contemporary Challenges* (Lanham: Lexington Books, 2017), 40.

49. Mfum-Mensah, *Education, Social Progress*, 40–1; Ministry of Education, data for the school year 2007/2008, https://www.unicef.org/wcaro/wcaro_GHA_MTSP2.pdf.

Chapter 3

Ghanaian Women and the International Migration Process

Until fairly recently, the literature on migration in Africa, including Ghana, was gendered male. Women were not regarded as able to make independent decisions to migrate and therefore not seriously considered in analyses of migration patterns. That trope on migration discourse reflected Africa's colonial past, an era during which European officials sent men to work in mines and on plantations while women were encouraged or sometimes forced, with the help of traditional male authority figures, to stay at home. Thus, when scholars wrote about migration as a male phenomenon, they were reflecting the reality of the nature of migration in some African societies. There has been a shift in approach in the literature and migrant women are now considered a distinct category of analysis. What is emerging from this new literature is that women migrate for the same reasons as men do, in response to crises and for better economic and/or educational opportunities. With reference to Ghanaian women, a complex but also interesting scenario comes into play. They tend to travel independently when they travel within the West African sub-region.[1] One can surmise that their independent migration in the sub-region results from the short distances they have to travel, the relatively cheaper costs of travel, and the absence of visa requirements to enter other West African countries due to protocols of the Economic Community of West African States. Women's international migration (i.e., migration outside the continent), on the other hand, has been more complicated, involving both dependent and independent immigrants in time and space. I examine these dynamics in the sections that follow.

Obtaining statistics on Ghanaian international migration generally is a difficult undertaking, and difficult still when gender is factored into the search. From 1874 to 1957 Ghana was a British colony. Its colonized status meant that it could not establish diplomatic relations with other countries on its own behalf. The implication then was that Ghanaians desiring to travel abroad would have had to do so as British subjects. Unfortunately, I could not uncover statistics that showed Ghanaian immigrants as British subjects traveling to international destinations prior to independence. However, there are scattered references to men who went abroad to study before and during the colonial period. They include Jacobus Capitein, a Fanti man sold as a slave when he was only seven years and educated by his master at Leyden University in the Netherlands, where he graduated in 1742;[2] there was also James Kwegyir Aggrey, another Fanti who obtained a doctorate in divinity from Hood Theological Seminary in North Carolina in 1912 and a teacher's certificate from Columbia University in 1918. Aggrey became a great scholar and pastor in the US and Ghana. He is credited with the saying that when you educate a woman, you educate a nation,[3] a radical thought indeed given his time and nature of British education in colonial Ghana that privileged the education of boys over girls. Perhaps the most famous of these early travelers was Kwame Nkrumah, the first president of Ghana, who studied in Pennsylvania at Lincoln University and the University of Pennsylvania and engaged in some political organizing of African students from 1935 to 1945 before returning to Ghana.[4] I did not uncover a record of a woman who went overseas to study, nor is there a record that says the aforementioned men took women along with them. Capitein traveled as a young boy, Aggrey married an African American woman and Nkrumah married an Egyptian woman after his studies in the US.

The post-independence period ushered in increased Ghanaian international migration but the pattern continued to be that of mostly male students who studied principally in Britain.[5] Again, men dominated this migration pattern because of the relatively low levels of female education during the colonial period. It is safe to say that early female migrants were wives. They might have been listed as dependents (since they were not principal applicants); however, such a designation would have masked their role as principal supporters of the male students. Women who accompanied male students as spouses worked to pay the bills as their husbands studied full-time. By the late-1960s, the trend was beginning to change. More and more women were receiving higher education in Ghana, albeit in smaller numbers compared with men. A small number of these educated women traveled abroad as students.[6] Then Nigeria's economy took an upswing in the 1970s and changed Ghana's immigration history, including the immigration of women.

The discovery of oil in Nigeria in 1956 led to dramatic economic growth that peaked in the mid-1970s. Both the private and public sectors in Nigeria needed middle-level professionals to work in the expanding economy while increasing wealth created avenues for unskilled workers to pick up work that Nigerians may not do. Just about the time that Nigeria's economy was booming, Ghana's was in decline. Economic decline coupled with a succession of military interventions in government led to a state of hardship and insecurity in Ghana. "Agege," as Nigeria came to be called, presented an economic pull that people in the West African sub-region took advantage of. Of the millions of migrants who flocked into Nigeria, Ghana seems to have sent the most people. Estimates of Ghanaians in Nigeria at the time of an expulsion order that was issued in January 1983 ranged from 300,000 to 3 million.[7] The migrants comprised men and women from rural and urban areas. The kinds of jobs that were in demand in Nigeria were also ones that favored women in Ghana. Teaching and nursing offered professional women an avenue in Nigeria to improve upon their economic circumstances. For unskilled women, commercial sex became an attractive option. Traders who lost their capital during the Rawlings intervention also saw an opening to work and build capital with which to restart their businesses. Thus, for the first time, Ghanaian women traveled as independent economic migrants in large numbers.

Migrants returned from Nigeria with material things that were usually associated with city life or persons of means. This may sound amusing to people who may not be familiar with the social and economic contexts in rural areas in Ghana in the mid-1970s, when the exodus to Nigeria began, but things that were considered out of reach for average folks—sound systems, suitcases, even hot water flasks—were tantalizingly displayed by migrants returning from Nigeria. In fact, those of us who lived in rural communities at the time were curious, when a migrant arrived from Nigeria, to see how they looked, what they brought, the stories they told, and the possibility that they might offer to take some of us along when they went back. Stories abounded of people using all manner of ways to get out of Ghana and into Nigeria. We heard stories of mothers who sneaked out at night while their children slept, of students absconding with tuition fees, or of a mourning family learning that money set aside to buy a coffin for a deceased member had been used by one of their own to go to Nigeria. While such stories could not be corroborated, they created an almost magical aura of travel to Nigeria and the potential payoff. The stories of desperate Ghanaians using any available means, however reckless, to go to Nigeria reflected an economic/materialist basis of migration common to people everywhere who want to improve their lives by moving to places of economic advantage. According to Micah Bump, about two million Ghanaians migrated between 1974 and 1981, the majority ending up in Nigeria.[8]

However, Nigeria was not the economic haven that many Ghanaians thought it was. The social conditions did not appear to be favorable to female migrants; in fact, some women deemed the conditions dangerous. Commercial sex workers were particularly susceptible to attacks. They complained of employers not paying them or paying them less than they were due[9]; of murder of sex workers, and of general hostility toward migrants, particularly in 1983 during the expulsion order.[10] Perhaps as a result of their experiences, many Ghanaians in Nigeria, including women, started looking farther afield for better economic conditions and personal security. Some returned to Ghana, others to other African states, while still others eyed Europe, particularly West Germany. After World War II, West Germany adopted a policy of providing refuge for people fleeing oppressive regimes. It operated that system from 1949 and revised the policy only in 1993 to cut back on the number of people entering the country to claim asylum.[11] The problem for the Ghanaians was that they could not technically claim refugee status in West Germany or any other European country for that matter. The 1951 United Nations Convention on Refugees (UNHCR) and its accompanying 1967 Protocol that established the definition of a refugee also recognized safe third country settlement of refugees.[12] The implication for the Ghanaians was that Nigeria was a safe third country if they went there because of persecution or the fear thereof. But the Ghanaians had an alternative; they could circumvent the provisions of the Refugee Convention and accompanying Protocol by turning to Article 14 (a) of the United Nations Declaration of Human Rights that states that it is a human right for people to seek protection in other countries if they were persecuted.[13] Article 14 (a) created an asylum category that was favorable to Ghanaians wishing to enter West Germany. Unlike refugees, asylum seekers must present themselves at the gate of the country in which they desire to seek protection. That means that an asylum seeker must pay upfront, from their own resources, the cost of travel. Fortunately, Nigeria had given Ghanaian migrants the financial resource to make the trip abroad.

As straight forward as the language of the UN Declaration on asylum is, its application is a little bit convoluted. The onus rests on the asylum seeker to prove that she or he has been persecuted. The Ghanaians in Nigeria could point to the revolution in Ghana to make a case for political persecution; similarly, their expulsion from Nigeria could mean that it could no longer be considered a safe third country.

The situation for Ghanaians at home in Ghana who wanted to travel abroad was different. They bore the brunt of the economic hardship and political insecurity unleashed by Rawlings. They had legitimate claims to asylum if they could get out of the country. Their problem was that it was difficult in the revolutionary days to obtain travel documents without which one could not travel abroad. There was only one passport office in Ghana in the early 1980s and it was located in Accra. The number of offices has since increased but as late as 2013, the *Al-Hajj* newspaper reported that the main office in Accra and its regional operation centers were in complete disarray. They could not coordinate their activities and that had resulted in a huge backlog. If that was happening in

2013, one can imagine how it was like to obtain a passport in the heyday of the revolution in the early 1980s. People living outside Accra had to make the trip, join long queues, and hope that they would have their turn. If they did not have family or friends in Accra, they would have to find accommodation. It took several months for a passport to be issued, and during the period, an applicant could make several follow-up trips to Accra. The incidental cost of obtaining a passport alone could be far greater than the actual cost of getting one.

If obtaining a passport was difficult, so also was securing a visa. The process was simply intimidating. Like the passport office, all foreign embassies are located in Accra. The "foreignness" of the process and possibility of denial could make people nervous when they appeared for interviews. Some people simply could not think of going through the process themselves. This is where "connection" came into play. Connection involved a network of people who helped potential immigrants to travel to countries abroad where it would be difficult for the immigrants to enter on their own merit.[14] Connection even engendered new ways of expression. Connection men (but not connection women) could "read the connection" to determine the possibility of landing a client in a particular country to "eat medicine," ergo, claim asylum. It was through connection that people came to know about West Germany as a popular destination for asylum seekers.[15]

Connection was both expensive and risky. Being able to read the connection, obtain a passport and visa was only the beginning of a long and complicated process. The connection man also had to craft a script of persecution or fear of persecution that would sound credible to immigration officials. The potential immigrant had to memorize the script and be consistent in its telling. The most crucial aspect of connection was the ability of the connection man to successfully land the immigrant in the destination country. Sometimes things did not go as planned and a potential immigrant was deported back to Ghana. In such situations, the immigrant lost everything and might not be able to raise enough funds to start the immigration process all over again.

Connection was highly risky and only the strong-hearted ventured in it. But people ventured. As late as 1997, a Ghanaian woman's story became headline news in the US when she was arrested by the Immigration and Naturalization Service (INS). She had claimed in her asylum hearing that she was next in line to be queen mother of her town but had broken certain traditional rules for which she feared she would undergo genital cutting. She told the hearing: "I will be mutilated, and my lover will be found and executed. After that, I will have to live the rest of my life in shame."[16] This powerful affidavit came under INS suspicion and the woman was arrested. The arrest brought out important people, powerful feminists, and human rights activists including the then first lady Hillary Clinton and actress Julia Roberts in defense of the woman. Meanwhile, the chief of the woman's alleged hometown flew to New

York to testify against her. Afterwards he issued a strong-worded statement condemning the woman for lying. Among other things, the chief stated,

> As a matter of fact, we Fantes do not practice female genital mutilation either as a custom, or as a way of punishing anybody. We are peace-loving people who believe in the sanctity of human beings, and I cannot imagine anybody slandering Ghanaians for a practice that is foreign to my tribe. I do not wish for her to be punished for blasphemy, but I take exception to a lie of this magnitude, where a whole community and country are portrayed as cannibals.[17]

Strong words, but that case was not an isolated case. A similar one happened in Toronto when a Ghanaian man told Canadian immigration officers that his father, who was a chief, had passed away and tradition demanded human sacrifice before his father would be buried. He was the first son and the one to be sacrificed, and that was the reason he fled Ghana. When that story broke, it enraged the Ghanaian immigrant community in Toronto to an extent that the man's lawyer used the community's anger to argue for a stay of deportation since the anger in Canada would likely be replicated in Ghana with potentially serious consequences for the man.[18] These kinds of stories prompted the government of Ghana and the Ghanaian media to put out advertisements to warn people about the risks of connection. Men who had never traveled abroad and had no knowledge of how immigration systems worked in various European countries preyed on innocent and desperate Ghanaians and duped them of large sums of money by posing as connection men. Even genuine connection men (those who were able to successfully land immigrants in destination countries) could create problems for immigrants. In certain situations they would change a person's identity by assigning her or him a new name, age, and nationality to match the characteristics that destination countries desired or required. Thus, a twenty-five-year-old immigrant could be carrying a passport that said he or she was forty years.[19] Such situations held long-term health and retirement implications if the immigrant secured admission. Above all, the possibility of deportation held serious financial and emotional issues for would-be immigrants. But in the heat of wanting to travel abroad, these warning signs did not deter potential immigrants.

That people would knowingly participate in a highly risky process such as connection pointed to the desperation of Ghanaians to escape hardships unleashed by a failing economy and the difficulty of legally entering Western countries of their choice on their own merit. Indeed, when we think about it, connection bore the hallmarks of human trafficking as defined by the UN Office of Drugs and Crime (UNODC). Trafficking refers to

> the recruitment, transportation, transfer, harbouring or receipt of persons, by means of the threat or use of force or other forms of coercion, of abduction,

> of fraud, of deception, of the abuse of power or of a position of vulnerability or of the giving or receiving of payments or benefits to achieve the consent of a person having control over another person, for the purpose of exploitation. Exploitation shall include, at a minimum, the exploitation of the prostitution of others or other forms of sexual exploitation, forced labour or services, slavery or practices similar to slavery, servitude or the removal of organs.[20]

Connection resembled trafficking in the key elements of fraud, deception, payments, and vulnerability. Connection men capitalized on the volatile economic and political climate in Ghana in the late 1970s and early 1980s to convince desperate, vulnerable, potential immigrants that they could deliver a service that the immigrants wanted. Their tactics could be fraudulent in the aspect of falsifying immigration documents; deceptive in regard to convincing potential immigrants of their ability to land the immigrants in destination countries, even if they couldn't; and also exploitative to the degree that they got huge payments that may not be commensurate with the services they provided. However, the definition of exploitation as defined in the UN protocol is nuanced within the framework of connection. In most cases, the connection man's work was done once the immigrant reached his or her destination. In that sense, the connection man had no say in the kind of work the immigrant engaged in or rights to the money the immigrant made. That is, unless the immigrant was a man. As we will see shortly, women were susceptible to sexual exploitation and abuse but mostly not at the hands of the connection men themselves. Women could be sexually exploited by first contacts in the destination country.

There is another area in which connection resembled trafficking but with its own twist. International human traffickers are usually part of organized crime rings that deal in drugs and guns and run business ventures that conceal their criminal activities.[21] Connection men, on the other hand, acted as "lone wolfs in concert." That is, they acted in their "areas of expertise" without necessarily coordinating with each other. They might not even know each other. For instance, one person might be good in procuring passports while another might be good at tampering with passports. The person obtaining the passport might not know what the passport holder did when he or she took delivery of the passport. The person who would fly out with the potential immigrant might not know how the immigrant obtained the passport but might know the person who tampered with it, or in some cases, he would be the "tamperer" and fly out person simultaneously. Thus, the complex nature of the phenomenon called connection did not fit neatly with the UN characterization of trafficking. In some specific ways, connection had a gender dimension, an issue that is explored next.

GENDER-SPECIFIC PROBLEMS OF MIGRATING

If there was a group of people in Ghana who had a greater need to migrate in the late 1970s and early 1980s, it would be women. They suffered some of the worst excesses of Rawlings's revolution. Business women saw their capital dwindle or businesses destroyed in the name of revolutionary house cleaning. Women who were employed by government suffered from SAPs through layoffs or nonpayment of salaries. Women in rural farming communities could benefit from international migration if they had the resources. Being the backbone of the subsistence economy in an era of structural adjustment and revolutionary insecurity, rural women bore the brunt of the worst aspects of the political economy. Unfortunately, they were also the least likely to be exposed to the processes of and requirements for international migration. For such women, marriage to a person already settled abroad was perhaps their best chance. If women had reasons to travel, migration posed gender-specific problems that were difficult to overcome. Even connection that appeared to be a gender-neutral process had gender-specific implications. A woman seeking to travel during the heyday of the revolution could potentially encounter financial difficulty and sexual exploitation at the hands of connection men. The expectation for sex increased when a potential female immigrant was single. Thus the problem of double exploitation—paying huge sums and/or having to give sex—became a deterrent for many women. A woman who lived in Germany before entering Canada in 1986 was candid about her experience with her connection man when she recounted her story:

> The moment we reached the airport [in Germany] the connection man told me his work was over, but he knew some friends who could help me. I needed to see those friends to get around, knowing that I did not speak German and my English was limited. The friends turned out to be one man, and he was willing to accommodate me on condition that I slept with him. Having very little choice, I stayed with this man for two weeks as an "asala"[22] after which time he sent me out to go and seek asylum. Obviously he had an endless supply of helpless Ghanaian women.[23]

Hers was not an isolated case. Stories reached Ghana through returning immigrants or letters that immigrants sent to their relatives about women who were mistreated by connection men. Instead of seeing those experiences in the context of the sexual exploitation of immigrant women, the stories were twisted and circulated in Ghana in exaggerated form. Exploited women were believed to engage in prostitution, a charge that carried social stigma even though prostitution was quite common, particularly in urban areas. To avoid exploitation and/or the charge of prostitution, some women sought out men who were already settled abroad to marry them so that they could immigrate as family class and avoid the hassle. Thus, to borrow Adepoju's words, some Ghanaian women became followers of men; however, Ghanaian women's decisions to migrate as spouses were not based on their spouses' migratory behavior. The women used men/marriage to make their own migration possible.

Another dimension to the immigration process that women experienced differently from men was in regard to immigration policies in receiving countries. The main reason that countries like Canada and the US, two of the major immigrant-receiving countries in the world, did not attract the Ghanaian immigrants in the initial stages of their increased international migration was because of the provisions in those countries' immigration policies. Both countries' immigration policies privilege skill and experience as conditions for the admission of independent immigrants. While skill and experience, which are outcomes of education, appear to be gender neutral, they have gender-specific outcomes. Skill and experience impose restrictions on the entry of immigrant women from countries where women's education lags behind men. And many of the Ghanaian women did not have the academic or professional qualifications that Canadian or US immigration policy required. Girls in Ghana had the advantage of free basic education as mandated by government in the post-independent era. However, tradition, geography, and poverty affected the number of girls who continued post-primary education.[24] And like most women elsewhere, Ghanaian women who received secondary and tertiary educations mostly ended up in traditionally feminized jobs—teaching, nursing, and secretarial work. Unfortunately, their expertise in these job areas were not what Canada or the US was looking for in the period under consideration.

If the women could not use their educational qualifications, there were other options that could facilitate their entry. Family reunification could work to their advantage as both the US and Canada had provisions for these in their immigration policies. But here again, the women did not seem to have a lot of luck. Family reunification worked if there was an established community of legal Ghanaian immigrants who could sponsor family members as allowed by immigration policy. That community was just not there or was so small that it could not have accounted for a perceptible increase in the number of Ghanaian immigrants in either country. Entering as refugees appeared to be the last best option for women migrating directly from Ghana. As already stated, they had suffered greatly during the Rawlings revolution and would have had the chance of claiming refugee status in either Canada or the US had the revolution drawn as much international attention and criticism as other political crises in Africa.[25] This appears to have been the case with Ghanaian refugees who entered the US. For the period that we have disaggregated data for refugees and asylees to the US, the figures for Ghana were very low. In fact, in some years the statistics did not have a single refugee/asylee entry from Ghana. Between 1990 and 2004, for example, only 40 people were admitted from Ghana.[26] At first glance it is easy for a person familiar with the political history of Ghana to conclude that Ghana returned to democratic governance in 1993; hence the basis for a person to claim political persecution was vastly decreased. Yet, it should be stressed that before 1990, Ghana did not appear in US refugee listings at all.

As a result of problems of entry into the US, Ghanaian immigrant women (and men) gravitated toward West Germany where they had a fair chance of entry. In his study of Ghanaian refugees in Canada, Opoku-Dapaah noted that there were nearly twenty thousand Ghanaians living in 17 European countries between 1988 and 1989.[27] However, West Germany did not provide women with the work environment that they might have anticipated. They were put in welfare communities and their movement restricted. They always had to carry travel documents with them to avoid being picked up and deported. Importantly, while they were allowed to stay in the country, they were not given permanent resident status that would have cleared the way for them to become citizens eventually. As a result of these measures, some decided to leave West Germany for other European destinations. England, France, and Holland became the favorite choices for the women,[28] possibly because of the ease with which they could find employment as cleaners, in the fast food industry, and for some, in the sex industry. Once settled in these countries, a small number of women began opening shops where they sold Ghanaian food items and other wares. Others took to sewing and hair braiding to serve the burgeoning Ghanaian immigrant communities. The enterprising character in the women did not die with the difficult immigration process.

Ghanaians who went to Europe before the events of 1979 and 1981 started visiting home at a time when many people were still going to Nigeria. European arrivals, especially those arriving from West Germany called borgers,[29] flaunted newly acquired wealth and confidence unmatched by those coming from Nigeria. Borgers arrived home with luxury items like latest model cars, and electrical and electronic appliances. They also brought new fashion trends—men wore their hair in jerry curls while women wore leather pants. Importantly, borgers brought "currencies that had weight"—US dollars and European currencies that had greater exchange value than the Nigerian naira. Borgers also started building large houses and taking care of family members. And because of their assumed wealth and financial support of family members, borgers became important power brokers in their families and communities regardless of their age or gender. That was a departure from established traditions. Age and gender were important markers of power in society. Generally, older men wielded power over women[30] (regardless of age) and younger men. Older men's power derived from their custody of family resources. Now, all of a sudden, younger people were coming home from abroad with resources that held greater value and significance than family resources that older men controlled. By virtue of their possession of certain assets, borgers assumed power that transcended established norms and traditions. Surely traveling abroad had a transformative quality that was not lost on people.

As already indicated, Ghanaians who traveled abroad before the mass migration of the late 1970s were mostly students (and their spouses). Students usually studied in Britain, Canada, and the US.[31] When students visited home they exhibited a different kind of immigrant lifestyle. Their outlook was decidedly professional, devoid of the ostentation characteristic of borgers. Students also returned after visiting Ghana. On the other hand, some borgers could not go back to the same countries in Europe after they visited home because they violated the terms of their refugee/asylee admission.[32] That limitation was a problem that they sought to avoid. Just as economic boom in Nigeria in the 1970s attracted Ghanaians to that country, so did a rumored change in immigration policy in Canada attract Ghanaians in Europe to Canada. Word got around in 1986 that Canada was in the process of reforming its immigration policy, part of which involved regularizing the status of undocumented immigrants by giving an "amnesty." Having learned a lesson or two in the art of connection, the Ghanaians in Europe began another migratory pattern. Both women and men presented themselves at the gate in Canada as refugees. Canadian refugee adjudication records are full of accounts of Ghanaian refugee claimants.[33] Thus began the increased migration of Ghanaians in Canada. Once they entered Canada, some found their way south, settling mostly in Washington, DC, and the Newark-New York metro area.

The comparison of US and Canadian immigration statistics is to illustrate the changing patterns of Ghanaian migration to North America. As the table shows, North America as a whole did not appear to be on the radar of Ghanaian immigrants prior to the mid-1980s. Before 1980, Africa supplied

Table 3.1 Ghanaian Immigrant Arrivals to Canada and the US, 1979–1985

Year	*Canada*	*US*
1979	137	0
1980	165	0
1981	198	0
1982	85	0
1983	134	0
1984	122	0
1985	194	0
1986	—	0
Total	1,035	0

Table 3.2 Ghanaian Immigrant Arrivals to Canada and the US, 1986–1992

Year	*Canada*	*US*
1986	234	1,164
1987	956	1,120
1988	387	1,239
1989	424	2,045
1990	444	3,330
1991	1,118	1,867
1992	2,451	1,604
Total	6,018	12,369

Source: Adapted from Employment and Immigration Canada, Immigration Statistics, 1986–1992; Department of Homeland Security, Yearbook of Immigration Statistics, 1986–1992.

the smallest number of immigrants to the US compared with immigrants from other major world regions[34]. However, as Table 3.2 shows, by the early 1990s, the trend was shifting and more and more Ghanaians started entering the US. Once admitted and their status legalized, this new group started sponsoring family members in a chain migration that continues to this day. The diversity lottery program has also contributed greatly to the number of Ghanaian immigrants in the US. Among African nationalities, Ghana is among the top ten countries that arrive in the US on diversity lottery visa. There has also been a trend among Ghanaians in Canada that they tend to move to the US to settle permanently but Ghanaians in the US do not usually move in the opposite direction. Table 3.2 shows that Ghanaian arrivals in the US started to pick up after 1985 and continued to do so well into the 2000s.

The American Community Survey data for 2010 showed that there were nearly 109,000 Ghanaians in the US, and 43% was women.[35] Listening to the women's narratives I could infer that a sizable proportion of women entering the US did so in the family category. They entered mainly as spouses. Some entered with the men at the same time while others arrived after the men had already settled. Women who entered in the family class category were listed in the immigration records as dependents, regardless of their ages.

Sponsored immigrants enjoy initial advantages that independents may not enjoy. For instance, sponsorship took the financial burden of international travel off the women's shoulders; sponsorship also meant that the women would not have to worry about accommodation or familiarizing themselves in their immediate neighborhoods. On the other hand, the very fact that such women were indebted to men for their entry into the US could create problems that independent immigrant women might not encounter. At the level of the state, sponsored immigrants could not access certain social programs such as public housing or financial assistance unless in extenuating circumstances. These are all important considerations when we examine the women's attitudes toward work.

In the meantime, though, the women finally found a home. For some, it had been a long and winding process—from Ghana to Nigeria, and then through several European destinations to Canada and finally to the US. For others, the process had proven arduous by the fact that they had to use connection men to get to the US. And still for others, the journey was smooth and straightforward because they were sponsored. Women's entry category had implications for their eventual adaptation, but much depended on their own agency in how they applied themselves in their new home.

NOTES

1. Charlotte Wrigley-Asante, "Survival or escaping poverty: the perspectives of poverty and well-being among Ghanaian women in cross-border trading," *Journal of Gender Studies* 22, no. 3 (2013):327–328, 320–334, http://dx.doi.org/10.1080/09589236.2012.703519.

2. Allison Blakely, Blacks in the Dutch World: The Evolution of Racial Imagery in a Modern Society (Bloomington: Indiana University Press, 1993); see also Nicholaus Wirth, "Capitein, Jacobus Elisa Johannes (1717?-1747)," *BlackPast.org*, http://www.blackpast.org/gah/capitein-jacobus-elisa-johannes-1717-1747#sthash.XQu9OpMa.dpuf.

3. Sankofa: Profile of Great African history maker -Dr. James Emmanuel Kwegyir Aggrey, http://sankofaonline.com/archives/9078.

4. Basil Davidson, *Modern Africa: A Social and Political History* (London: Longman, 1994), 137–8.

5. Valentina Mazzucato and Mirjam Kabki, "Small is Beautiful: The Micro-politics of Transnational Relationships between Ghanaian Hometown Associations and Communities Back Home," *Global Networks* 9, no. 2 (2009): 231.

6. Martha Donkor, "The Education of Immigrant Women: Prospects and Challenges for Ghanaian Immigrant Women in Canada," PhD diss., OISE/UT, 2000, 65.

7. See Johnson Olaosebikan Aremu, "Responses to the 1983 Expulsion of Aliens from Nigeria: A Critic," *African Research Review* 7, no. 3 (July 2013): 345; "Throwback Photos of Ghanaians being Deported from Nigeria in 1983," http://www.tori.ng/news/5806/see-historic-pictures-of-ghanaians-leaving-nigeria.html; Mazzucato and Mirjam Kabki, "Small is Beautiful," 231.

8. Micah Bump, "Ghana: Searching for Opportunities at Home and Abroad," Migration Policy Institute, March 1, 2006, http://www.migrationpolicy.org/article/ghana-searching-opportunities-home-and-abroad/.

9. Such stories need further scrutiny, especially against the backdrop of expectations from immigrants. A person who is unable to send material things home as expected may write home about the brutality of her Nigerian employers.

10. Beth Hart, "How Shehu Shagari Expelled a Million Ghanaians from Nigeria," https://www.naij.com/575451-photos-shehu-shagari-expelled-million-nigeria-consequences.html.

11. Freda Hawkins, *The Asylum Seekers* (Toronto: Canadian Institute of International Affairs, 1994), 8.

12. UNHCR, http://www.unhcr.org.

13. United Nations, *Universal Declaration of Human Rights,* http://www.un.org/en/universal-declaration-human-rights/index.html.

14. Donkor, "Marching to the Tune," 32–3.

15. Donkor, "Marching to the Tune," 33.

16. Francie Grace, "Mutilation Horror, or Hoax?" *CBS News*, January 14, 2003, http://www.cbsnews.com/news/mutilation-horror-or-hoax; see also William Branigin and Douglas Farah, "Asylum Seeker is Imposter, INS Says," *Washington Post,* December 2000, posted with permission by the University of Maryland, http://jclass.umd.edu/archive/newshoax/casestudies/idfraud/IDAsylum3.html.

17. Accra Mail, "We are not Savages—Chief Nana Kwa Bonko V," Ghanaweb, January 19, 2003, http://www.ghanaweb.com/GhanaHomePage/NewsArchive/We-Are-Not-Savages-Chief-Nana-Kwa-Bonko-V-31766.

18. Personal conversation with attorney Charles Anipare in Toronto, December 3, 1996.

19. Personal conversation with Ghanaian refugee claimant in Toronto, December 3, 1996.

20. UNODC, "Human Trafficking," http://www.unodc.org/unodc/en/human-trafficking/what-is-human-trafficking.html.

21. UNODC, "Human Trafficking."

22. "Asala" was the corrupted form of asylee, as used by Ghanaian immigrants in West Germany.

23. Quoted in Donkor, "Marching to the Tune," 33.

24. Felix Odei-Akuffo, "Teenage Pregnancies and School Dropouts: The Relevance of Family Life Education and Vocational Training to Girls Employment Opportunities," in *Sex Roles, Population and Development in West Africa,* Christine Oppong, ed., (London: James Currie, 1987), 157.

25. Opoku-Dapaah, "Decade of Repression," 10; see also Mazzucato and Kabki, "Small is Beautiful," 231.

26. Department of Homeland Security, Immigration Data and Statistics, "Refugees and Asylees Data Tables, Refugee Arrivals into the United States by region and Country of Chargeability, Fiscal Years 1990–2004, Table 15."

27. Opoku-Dapaah, *The Adaptation of Ghanaian Immigrants in Toronto* (North York: York Lanes Press, 1993), 18.

28. Mazzucato and Kabki, "Small is Beautiful," 230–1.

29. I do not know exactly when the word came into popular usage, but by the mid-1980s, it was used to describe Ghanaians arriving from Europe. The word is gender neutral and is used to apply to both women and men (interestingly, Ghanaians who were expelled from Nigeria were called "returnees").

30. Elderly women acquired prestige by virtue of their age but that did not necessarily translate into power over others.

31. Mazzucato and Kabki, 231–2.

32. Refugees and asylees who go back to their countries of origin when their cases are still pending would not have legal papers for reentry. See *Karikar*i v. Canada (Minister of Employment and Immigration*)* (1994), 169 N.R. 131 (F.C.A.).

33. *Karikari* v. Canada (Minister of Employment and Immigration) (1994), 169 N.R. 131 (F.C.A.).
34. U.S Census Bureau, American Community Survey, 2010, https://www.census.gov/prod/2012pubs/acs-19.pdf.
35. American Community Survey, 2010.

Chapter 4

The Chance and Choice of Live-in Caregiving

In 2009, when I started researching the lives of Ghanaian immigrant live-in caregivers, the Great Recession was in full swing. Thousands of Americans were losing their jobs on a daily basis. However, a sizable number of Ghanaian women (and some men) in New York City were gainfully employed as caregivers in various capacities and others were contemplating taking up jobs in the sector. And so I wondered. Did the women make the decision to become caregivers based on the availability of jobs in that sector? Were they pushed into the sector because of their gender and status as immigrants? Did they come to the US specifically to work in the domestic sector, and hence following their career path? As I talked to the women about these questions, I gained insights that led me to conclude that live-in caregiving presented opportunities that the Ghanaian women could not ignore. Apart from giving them financial capital, the job also served as escape or sanctuary for women who had problems of one kind or another.

Before I analyze the concepts of escape or sanctuary as used in this chapter, it is important that I situate live-in caregiving within the larger realm of domestic work in both its paid and unpaid dimensions. When contextualized, it becomes evident that there is something interesting about American women's relationship to domestic work. In spite of their increasing participation in the paid labor force, and also the fact that men are now increasingly sharing in the performance of domestic work, American women continue to be primarily responsible for domestic chores.[1] They cook, clean, do the dishes, do the laundry, make the bed, do groceries, take care of children and the sick; in short, women's efficient running of the home ensures the health and comfort of members of the household. Women's domestic work also releases men to work full-time while also saving government at all levels the cost of providing care in some situations. This is not suggesting that the work men do at home is not essential; rather, men's domestic chores are not characterized by the same level of regimentation and repetition that characterize women's work at home. There is therefore no question of the value of domestic work to family life and the economy as a whole; there is also no question that women of all races perform domestic work. Yet, when the same work moves from unpaid housework to paid work in the market place, it loses value and respect in the popular psyche. It also ceases to be work done by women of all races; it becomes the work done by immigrant women of color. And so the question is why? Why immigrant women, and why immigrant women of color?

The lack of value and respect, and domination of domestic work by immigrant women of color has deeper roots in race relations in this country. Before immigrant women from Asia, the Caribbean, Central and South America, and Mexico took over paid domestic work, the sector was the special preserve of African American women until World War I.[2] White women too did paid domestic work but they did while searching for better alternatives. African American women did not have that option; they did domestic work from the days of slavery until the early twentieth century. And there, to me, lies the secret behind the undervaluation and less respect associated with domestic work.[3] African American women historically suffered extreme racism, classism, and sexism. From the days of slavery through Jim Crow, they worked in the homes of middle and upper-class white Americans for no pay or for very little pay. Slave women who lived and worked in the big house not only suffered sexual abuse at the hands of masters and their sons, but they also had to contend with the extreme jealousy and anger of plantation wives who did not seem to have answers to their husbands' philandering. Plantation wives could spit on and/or beat domestic slaves or sell their children as punishment.[4] Domestic slaves who internalized the ill-treatment came to be known as mammy—docile, selfless, non-threatening, hardworking women—and were the ones that were desired. The opposite of the mammy was the Jezebel and she was the least desired.[5]

The utter disrespect, devaluation, indeed dehumanization of African American women seemed to have transferred to their work and created an image of domestic work as work for the downtrodden. This was particularly the case in the South. Even after the Civil War, the new middle class sought to apply the old regime of strict control that they established during slavery to free African Americans generally, and African American women in paid domestic work, in particular.[6] For instance, a post–Civil War South Carolina law concerning domestic service stated that "Servants … in all the domestic duties of the family shall at all hours of the day and night and on all days of the week promptly answer all calls and obey and execute all lawful orders and commands of the family in whose service they are employed."[7] This meant that African American domestic women were on call 24 hours a day, seven days a week. Some white women did not even offer to pay cash for the women's services. Rather, the white employers gave their African American employees "toting privileges," that is, leftover food and used clothing in lieu of cash payment.[8] Employers who paid their domestic employees paid such small amounts that some African American families were glad to receive toting privileges.[9] Due to the hardship that women in domestic work faced, they quickly left whenever more "respectable" work opened up. Women who continued to work refused to live in, preferring rather to live out so they could escape the constant scrutiny and also have time for their own family responsibilities.[10] When the women left paid domestic work they left behind the low value, lack of dignity, and the culture of mistreatment associated with the work. Incidentally, the women who filled the vacuum created by African American women were not very different in terms of racial and cultural characteristics. They were black and brown women from poor countries. In a country like the US where skin color determines opportunities and one's worth as a worker is calculated in monetary terms, we get a convoluted equation of domestic work with the people who do the work. Thus, it was not because paid domestic work was women's work that gave it a poor image in American society; it was because it was predominantly the work of a certain kind of woman, the black (and brown) woman.[11]

THE CHANCE TO DO HOME CARE

Despite its poor public image, private care work is essential work. Government welcomes it to the extent that it reduces expenditure on the provision of care services for certain segments of the population; families need it due to the demands of modern work; and upper-class families with excess income to spend want it to relieve their women of housework drudgery. Other categories of people that have patronized domestic work in the US include diplomats and officials of international organizations.[12] To satisfy the domestic needs of these latter groups, the US government issues special visas, A-3 visas to domestic workers hired by diplomats and G-5 visas to those hired by other officials.[13] Experts generally agree that the demand for and supply of domestic care workers is the result of the creation of global inequality by capitalist globalization, although there are culturally specific factors that may have nothing to do with globalization or combine with the effects of globalization to create more inequality.[14] Women from poor countries in the Global South who are often the worst victims of the forces of globalization have capitalized on the same phenomenon and engaged in migration as part of a process that Barbara Ehrenreich and Arlie Russell Hochschild call "a worldwide gender revolution."[15] This global revolution entails women's agency in providing for themselves and their children in the absence of men or where there are men in their lives, to supplement the men's wages. Yet, "Third World immigrant women achieve their success only by assuming the cast-off roles of middle- and high-income women in the First World," note Ehrenreich and Hochschild.[16] What appears as patriarchal benevolence, that is, First World countries opening their gates to Third World women to "achieve their success," is actually part of a long history of First World exploitation of Third World women's labor. Understood from this perspective, it is not surprising that Third World women have come to dominate paid care work.

But that is not all. The chance for immigrant women to do domestic care work in the US correlates with the expansion in the sector, which is also a factor of the diversity in the sector. Immigrant women may care for children, elderly persons, sick or disabled family members, or be general house help who do the repetitive daily chores associated with family life. Women may also work in less isolated sites like hospitals, hotels, restaurants, and schools where they perform the dirtiest but essential services that ensure the health and comfort of patrons of these institutions. All these different forms of care work have their unique characteristics, even though they are linked together by the people who perform the services.

The expansion in the home care sector is not the result of increased migration of women of color into the US; it is rather because of the expansion in the home care sector that has occasioned the increased immigration of women of color. Three factors explain the expansion in the home care sector: advances in medical science and technology, women's increased labor force participation, and the cost of obtaining care. First, Americans are living longer because of improvements in the quality of life and decrease in the mortality rate.[17] Non-communicable and infectious diseases like diabetes and respiratory diseases that used to be big killers have been brought under reasonable control while rising incomes for the middle class has led to smarter life choices. The result has been a general state of longevity.[18] The baby boomer generation provides a good example for this phenomenon. Baby boomers, those who were born immediately after World War II, are now in their early seventies and retired or on their way to retirement. A CBS feature on this "great generation" sheds light on how they provide the impetus for the expansion of domestic care work. The article details that:

> In 1946, 3.4 million babies were born in the U.S ... Now, with the first of them turning 60, the baby boomers are going to retire from the workforce ... Boomers are expected to live longer than any previous generation of Americans. Of the 3.4 million born in 1946 … 2.8 million are still alive… By 2030, when the first baby boomers reach 84, the number of Americans over 65 will have grown by 75% to 69 million. That means more than 20% of the population will be over 65, compared with only 13% today.[19]

That article appeared in 2006. Six years later in 2012, the Department of Labor listed domestic work among the top ten fastest-growing sectors of the economy and projected that the sector will continue to grow into 2022. Debra Auerbach, a writer for CareerBuilder, even goes further. She predicts that the growth in the domestic care sector will continue well past 2022 as the number of people 65 and older is expected to hit 88.5m by 2050.[20]

As the table shows, the home care sector is projected to create more jobs than any other sector in the foreseeable future. The expansion in the population of seniors will open up more job opportunities in the care industry. As people grow older and become weak or suffer from age-related illnesses, they are going to need others to care for them, whether in institutionalized settings or in the privacy of their homes. Already, some elderly citizens, mostly white, upper middle-class men, have chosen to live in their own homes instead of going to retirement homes when they can no longer manage the basics of daily living. Unless they have family members who will care for them, these seniors are going to need paid caregivers. Ordinarily, women in their lives would be the care providers but as Ehrenreich and Hochschild note, upper- and middle-class white women have relinquished that responsibility to others beneath them in class.[21] Those "others" are immigrant women from mainly Third World countries.

Second, one can look to the dramatic increase in American women's education over the past forty years and its impact on women's labor force participation and incomes to understand the expansion in the domestic care sector. As more and more women obtain higher education, they enter the labor force, especially in professional fields where the demands of work keep them away from home.[22] Such women will need other women to do their housework. Similarly, as women's incomes rise due to their employment in the professions, they will relegate to others work that had been traditionally their preserve—housework. A White House white paper on women that was released in 2011 showed that the percentage of working mothers with children under eighteen years of age is steadily rising; however, the paper does not mention a corresponding provision of childcare services for such mothers.[23] What it means is that working mothers are going to need childcare services. Yet, cumbersome government policy on childcare leaves poor working families with children less option to afford care while increasing the chance for middle and upper income earners to be able to afford paid childcare.[24] But it is not only childcare that upper and middle-class families need. Their lavish lifestyles have also included hiring other people to do their dirty work at home.

Third, domestic service is cheap. As can be seen from Table 4.1 below, of all the fastest-growing jobs, personal care aide shows the strongest potential to grow and recruit a lot more people than the remaining top ten job areas combined. Yet, it is also the least remunerated on the list. With a mean

Table 4.1 The Ten Fastest-Growing Jobs, 2012–2022

Job	*Annual Median Salary*	*Projected Growth*
Industrial Organizational Psychologists	$80,330	53% (900 new jobs)
Personal Care Aides	$20,100	49% (580,800 new jobs)
Home Health Aides	$21,020	48% (424,200 new jobs)
Mechanical Insulation	$40,500	47% (13,500 new jobs)
Interpreters/Translators	$42,420	46% (13,300 new jobs)
Diagnostic Medical Sonographers	$66,410	46% (27,000 new jobs)
Masons' Helpers	$28,260	43% (10,500 new jobs)
Occupational Therapy Assistants	$55,270	43% (12,900 new jobs)
Genetic Counselors	$63,590	41% (900 new jobs)
Physical Therapist Assistants	$53,360	41% (49,400 new jobs)

Source: US Department of Labor Blog, March 15, 2015.

annual salary of $20,000, upper- and middle-class families can afford to hire women in the sector to care for their household needs. What has been happening then is that improved life expectancy, expansion in middle-class incomes, expansion in women's workforce participation, increase in the number of working mothers and affordable private care services have created a huge market for the domestic work sector. Women who want to care for children, seniors, disabled people, or be general house help have the chance to do so. And, if the current political rhetoric of demonizing, criminalizing, and targeting immigrants for deportations continues, its impact on the domestic job sector will be huge. Immigration, particularly from Third World countries where the greater majority of care workers come from, will taper off. Women in care work will demand more in better working conditions as a factor of demand and supply. We have not got to that point yet, but there is reason to believe that more and more middle and upper-class Americans are going to rely on caregivers.

We have already seen that African American women left the domestic work sector only when they had other job alternatives. Similarly, white women, whether immigrant or native-born, did domestic work as stop gap, a temporary measure to kill time as they looked for "real jobs." But that is only half the story. There is a reason why white women did not see paid domestic work as a job of choice. They had the opportunity to advance through education and onward to more job options in the market place. Significantly, white women have traditionally been the employers of domestic workers and know how they treat their workers. Having inside knowledge of the work conditions of domestic work, it is less likely that white women would encourage other whites, even if of a lower class, to enter the sector. This is not suggesting that there is a race conspiracy of white women against non-white women in the performance of domestic work for pay. Considering that paid domestic work has traditionally been equated with the people who do it and since domestic work was traditionally defined as black women's work, it follows then that white women, whatever their legal status, would not want to confuse their race (and class) with work that has been defined as "other racial." Is this a conscious thing that white women do, to shun domestic work? It is one of those normative things that put women in charge of certain roles and men in others. It is taken for granted and therefore validated. This is where immigrant women of color enter the conversation. Most enter the US from a position of weakness. They may not have the requisite education and skills to enter the formal sector and end up taking jobs in the care sector.

Ghanaian Women and the Choice of Care Work

The Ghanaian women were looking for better lives when they left Ghana. They also considered other destinations and ultimately decided that the US would offer them the best chance to achieve those lives. The women did not migrate specifically to work in the domestic care sector, as was the case with women from certain Asian and Latin American countries. What the Ghanaian women did was to make strategic decisions based on the dynamics of the economy at the time of their arrival and their own interests. The period of their increased entry into the US starting in the mid-1980s was an uncertain economic period. A recession in 1981–1982 and Reagan's supply-side economics in his first term drove up unemployment.[25] Women who arrived around that time talked of sometimes going for months without work and then when they did, it was as dish washers in fast food joints or cleaners in large stores. Then the Clinton years rolled in and manufacturing that had been the foundation of the economy gradually gave way to a technological, financial, and service culture that benefited those with expertise in technology and finance.[26] Unfortunately, the women had neither the training nor the expertise to take advantage of specialized jobs in the technology field. However, the economic boom of the era opened up more jobs in the service sector. Skilled personnel who had worked in the service sector because of the previous recession left the sector, thus creating openings for low-skilled personnel. The Ghanaian women indicated that they started entering the care sector in relatively large numbers in the 1990s.

It begs the question why the women would not retrain so that they could take advantage of better paying jobs in the technological and financial sectors, particularly given the economic conditions in Ghana that necessitated their immigration in the first place. In a study she did on Ghanaian women in Toronto, Martha Donkor offers insights that can help to explain why the women in New York did not enter school upon arrival in order to increase their economic value in the job market. Donkor notes that women mostly considered education and retraining after they had worked at several jobs and had been dissatisfied with those jobs. She also notes that the need to take care of pressing financial problems back in Ghana was a motivating factor for some women to start work as soon as they arrived in Canada.[27] Similar arguments could be made for the women in New York. Like their counterparts in Canada, they needed to work and did not discriminate among types of work, although as one of them said in her interview, "the work has to be honest labor." Honest labor meant that there were no shadowy dealings or questionable behaviors associated with the type of work. Even so, there is a belief among some Ghanaians that it is not the type of work that one does abroad that matters but what one is able to send home to Ghana. This "end justifies the means" perspective on Ghanaian immigrants' labor market participation calls to mind Goran Hyden's theory of the economy of affection.

According to Hyden, kinship ties and tribal obligations among peasants in Tanzania worked against their accumulation of capital that would have made it possible for them to develop a class-based society or a market economy.[28] Although a cultural, rather than an economic, construct, as Tony Waters observes,[29] the economy of affection can provide a lens through which one can view not tribal obligation, but community expectation as a reason for Ghanaian immigrants to start work immediately upon arrival in an immigration destination instead of enrolling in educational programs with long-term economic benefits. Ultimately, immigrants share their resources with their communities but sharing here does not mean that immigrants put their resources up for communal ownership and consumption. Individual immigrants accumulate wealth for themselves and members of their families. Sharing connotes a range of activities or provision of material goods by immigrants such as

a. building a modern house that beautifies and expands the size of the community
b. providing accommodation for needy family members
c. sending a vehicle home that can be commercialized for the benefit of the entire community
d. establishing a scholarship for poor students
e. building a school block for the community

An immigrant who provides any of these goods affirms her membership and affinity as a community member.[30] While not obligatory, people have come to expect that immigrants, more than non-immigrants, should "send modernity" to their communities. This expectation is based on the belief that immigrants have access to some resources that non-immigrants do not have access to. And given that government's development projects are slow to implement or not at all, especially in rural areas, rural communities in particular have mainly looked up to their "fortunate" members living abroad to bring development and enlightenment to their communities. Consequently, Ghanaian immigrants have developed a tradition of assuming partial responsibility for the development of their communities.[31] They send hospital equipment, computers, and money that runs into millions of dollars annually to family members and community elders for development.[32] When they improve the material conditions of their families and communities, immigrants enhance not just their status but also that of the families they belong to.[33] Indeed, in one of the regional capitals, Sunyani, and surrounding towns, there is an association of mothers of borgers. The members meet to talk about projects their children living abroad are undertaking; they also share stories about dishonest artisans and how to avoid them. Meeting time is also an occasion for the women to display their status as mothers of borgers. They wear expensive clothing and other accessories to match their status. These women have become "play man women" not by their own effort (although one can argue that they nurtured their children) but by having children living abroad. It reflects poorly on an immigrant whose mother is unable to join the group because the immigrant is not undertaking or has not undertaken a project in the community. It is also significant that the association is gendered female. The fact that mothers and not fathers (or mothers and fathers together) have formed this group suggests that mothers depend materially on their immigrant children more than fathers do. And in the Ghanaian case at least, it appears that mothers' dependence on daughters living abroad makes it easy for the daughters to send children home when it becomes necessary to do so. Thus, women's choice of live-in must be understood against the backdrop of pressure from the old country to prove that they were living in the US. They needed to work, and care work was readily available.

Despite the fact that the women made calculated decisions about their choice of work, observers who do not know the background in terms of expectations may conclude that their concentration in home-care work might be a sign of discrimination. For instance, when Ghanaians arrived in Toronto in large numbers starting from 1986, many immediately took to factory work and cab driving, even though some had degrees from universities in Ghana. A.B.K. Kasozi, a Ugandan immigrant activist and scholar in Toronto at the time referenced Ghanaian immigrants in particular to make the case that African immigrants were discriminated against in the Canadian job market.[34] While not challenging the merits of Kasozi's argument, it is also important to understand individual motivations and agency within a culture of discrimination; otherwise we risk seeing immigrants as perpetual victims. When there is intense pressure on immigrants to send material things to the country of birth, the question is not simply the job one deserves based on one's qualifications, but what is available for one to quickly acquire the material resources one needs. In most cases, when Ghanaian immigrants satisfy what I call "home needs" to a degree, they change jobs and other aspects of their lives in the destination country. They may go back to school, buy their own homes, and start sponsoring other family members. Until they satisfy those home needs, they may continue to work in areas that may appear less desirable, low waged, and a step down in status.[35] The women in this study calculated the merits of working in other areas vis-a-vis live-in caregiving and settled on the latter. These were their decisions, their choices even if the context within which they made those choices was racist and discriminatory.

So far the discussion has centered on cultural, institutional, and personal perspectives that drove women's decisions toward jobs in home care. There are other less obvious factors that influenced the women's choice of home care. We should note that immigrants are not promised jobs as a precondition for admission unless they enter the US on contract or on special visas to fill certain positions. Immigrants who join an already-established community of people from their country of origin enjoy advantages that enhance their labor market participation. This is especially the case for immigrants who enter in the family class category, having been sponsored by people who are already legally settled. The Ghanaian women arrived mostly in the family class category as wives whose husbands had been in the US for a while. Their arrival also coincided with a burgeoning Ghanaian immigrant community that afforded members the chance to network. Ghanaian immigrants tended to live in clusters, in the same apartment buildings in the same neighborhoods, notably Brooklyn, the Bronx, and Queens. In these settings, the husbands introduced their newly arrived wives to American life from a Ghanaian perspective in a way that would not be possible for, say, a student who arrived from Ghana and settled in a predominantly white neighborhood to attend a predominantly white university. What I am saying is that sponsored immigrants are more likely to quickly integrate into an existing immigrant community than independent immigrants. And when there is an existing community to integrate into, immigrants end up having choices. They get to hear about what is trending as well as minimizing their feelings of isolation and loneliness. When new immigrants know where to go and what to do, they make decisions that accord with their sense of agency—what they must do to make it in their new home. For the Ghanaian women, choosing live-in caregiving was thoughtfully carried out, as will be shown later in the book.

One of the major questions I asked the women was why they chose live-in, not as an economic question alone, which was obvious, but also as a gendered and racial question informed by African American women's historical connections to domestic work and its racial and gendered implications. Nearly all the women said they did not know that African American women had historically been connected to domestic work, an admission that made sense given the educational backgrounds of the women. Also, the women did not think that what happened to African American women in their job options in the past would necessarily determine how other black women would experience their work lives. The women rather suggested that racism *probably* had something to do with African American women working predominantly in the domestic work sector. In a rather bizarre submission, two women indicated that there is discrimination in every country against certain groups of people. The implication of the women's perspective was that it was unfortunate that African Americans became the group that was targeted for discrimination. The women's view on African American women's historical connection to domestic work answered one key question of the study—they did not think that they were pushed into live-in because they were black. In fact, they did not believe they were pushed into live-in at all. They chose to work in private care among a range of options that they could have pursued. Interestingly, the so-called range of options revolved around domestic service or other low-paying jobs in factories or as store clerks. One of the women explained that "When you go to someone else's country, you do not expect to be treated in the same way as the citizens of that country. You know why you went there, and you don't allow things that you cannot change to stand in the way of what you can possibly achieve."

Without appearing to do so, the woman admitted that there is racism in American society that can constrain one's chances; however, by framing her view on racism the way she did, she distinguished the Ghanaian women from African American women by invoking their immigrantness and thus symbolically placing themselves outside of the institutional structures that constrained the lives of African American women. There are two other ways that the woman's observation captured the collective thinking of the others in the study. First, the women took a practical approach to what they could expect as immigrants and put a positive spin on the job options available to them. They did not think that doing certain kinds of work was demeaning. They suggested that it is possible to work within racism by pretending that it did not exist. This accommodationist attitude might explain why they embraced their job opportunities without thinking about the context within which the jobs were offered. As far as they were concerned, it was simply a question of the economy and what was available. That way of thinking recalls an observation that Anita Ilta Garey and Karen Hansen made about discrimination broadly. They wrote, "Much of the discrimination argument rests on how broadly we define discrimination or on how trained the eye is on seeing it. Women have acclimatized themselves to discrimination, expect it, get it, and try to move around it."[36] One only has to recall the economic and political contexts the women lived in prior to their migration and their views on racism will make sense. As products of their culture, the Ghanaian women understood American culture by interpreting the latter through their own cultural grid. It is this layered process of thinking, of making sense of a foreign culture that created what might appear to others as an ignorant, accommodationist attitude toward racism.

Second, the woman's reference to "someone else's country" suggested that they did not see the US as a permanent place of residence, regardless of their legal status. They were in the US for a purpose—to acquire money and things that such money would buy to make their eventual return to Ghana comfortable and meaningful. By thinking that this is not their permanent home, they figuratively placed themselves on the margins of society, and that was a dangerous place to be in a country where marginalization occurs along the lines of skin color, gender, and other axes of exclusion. And yet the notion that they were immigrants and would return to their country of origin at some point is not unique to the Ghanaian women. It is an enduring theme that appears in discourse on immigrant settlement and adaptation in many places.

Philomena Essed was the first person I know who took a closer look at immigrants' views on permanently returning to their country of origin at some point when she studied the settlement and adaptation patterns of Guyanese immigrants in Holland. Essed noticed that the immigrants initially thought of themselves as transients in Holland; they would return to their homeland at a future date. Yet the exigencies of life in a foreign country did not always favor permanent return, and thoughts of going home eventually subsided.[37] Donkor applied the framework to the settlement patterns of Ghanaian immigrants in Toronto and arrived at similar conclusions. Many started off with the intention of living in Canada for a certain number of years and then going back to Ghana. However, as the years passed by, the resolve to go back gave way to a desire to go back which in turn gave way to the hope that one day they would go back to the old country.[38] A similar pattern seemed to characterize the thinking of the women in this study. They expressed the hope of resettling in the homeland in the future, although they admitted that their children would likely not go to settle in Ghana permanently. In preparation for this future relocation the women invested heavily in projects in Ghana. For the women to undertake their projects, they had to have unobstructed access to income. Live-in care work seemed to them a way to satisfy their goals.

Live-in as Escape or Sanctuary

It is clear that the availability of jobs in the domestic work sector was a major reason for Ghanaian immigrant women to seek out jobs as live-in caregivers.

However, that was only part of the story. Another dimension to their choice of care work revolved around their entry status. As already indicated, the women arrived in different categories of admission with implications for family life and job choice. Four of the women arrived as visitors and then stayed and took up jobs as caregivers. For these women, the intention was clear. They needed capital for one thing or other in Ghana. However, they could not raise the amount of money they needed because of their legal status. They had only two options. They could apply to live here permanently or work underground. This is where live-in served as a means of escape as illustrated with the story of Lydia.[39]

Lydia was getting ready to go to Ghana when I met her. She was in her late fifties and had been in the US for six years, four of those years as an undocumented live-in caregiver. She entered the US legally on a visitor's visa, having been sponsored by her daughter to care for her grandchildren as she did live-in. Lydia was excited about her sponsorship because she would meet her grandchildren for the first time and also experience the US firsthand. She had heard so much about the US and was eager to see and experience the country herself. Before she left Ghana she ran a successful building materials store that she arranged for her son to manage in her absence. Lydia's background undercuts the popular belief that immigrant caregivers were poor in their countries of origin.[40] Immigrant women may come from poor countries and may become poor in the US by virtue of losing their class position but their poverty in home countries is not a universal phenomenon. Lydia was a self-made businesswoman who enjoyed high status in her community. Chandra Mohanty has criticized the view of the so-called poor Third World woman by Western scholars. She cautions against essentializing Third World women as an undifferentiated category without regard to cultural contexts that produce different kinds of femininities.[41] We have already seen that one had to have a lot of money to be able to travel abroad from Ghana. We can extrapolate that unless they were sponsored on contract or lived in close proximity and would not pay much to travel to the US, immigrant women who entered the US independently cannot be assumed to have been poor in their countries of origin simply because they are women from poor countries.

In the US, Lydia took care of her two grandchildren and then a neighbor's child for free. In fact, she appeared surprised when asked why she babysat the neighbor's child free of charge. She knew of a Ghanaian grandmother who took money from her daughter for taking care of the grandchildren and was perplexed by that. She asked, "Who does that? I would not have accepted payment even if the mother had offered." Lydia was expressing deep-seated cultural norms about neighbors being each other's keeper. She considered the woman whose child she cared for not just as a neighbor, but family. That was how she knew life growing up in a small town in Ghana. She was grateful that her daughter had given her the opportunity to visit the US, although in reality, the daughter brought her to avoid sending her children to Ghana. Yet, Lydia believed that her daughter had done her a great favor and the least she could do was to show kindness to someone else. Besides, she knew that when it was time to go back to Ghana her daughter and the neighbor would reward her handsomely. Lydia also entertained the hope that her daughter would follow the example of other Ghanaians who invite their parents here and organize a grand send-off party in their parents honor. Some of these parties attract large crowds and the organizers make a lot of money. That was Lydia's hope.

A few months before she was scheduled to depart, Lydia's son who was running the store in Ghana called to inform her that he had arrived in the US. He had hired someone to run the store and used part of the capital to make the trip. All of a sudden Lydia faced a dilemma. Should she go back to Ghana as planned or risk overstaying her visa so she could work? How was she going to live if she went back, sensing that her business had collapsed? She did not even know the person her son hired to take care of the store, if indeed he hired someone. And much as she hoped her daughter would organize a send-off party at the end of her stay, she could not put all her hopes in a party that had not yet happened or how much people might donate when it was organized. If these were difficult questions, a more pressing one was deciding not to go to Ghana when her visa expired. She could apply to renew her visa but what would she do if she was denied? At fifty-three years Lydia did not think that she was strong enough to do any back-breaking job if she got one. She thought of informing her neighbors about babysitting but she had already set a precedent of babysitting one child for free. Above all, she worried that if she overstayed her visa, she could jeopardize a future chance of reentering the US. These were pertinent issues that demanded immediate answers.

Lydia decided that she would go back to Ghana at the end of her two years' legal residence to assess the state of her business. Then she got good news. A live-in caregiver needed someone to replace her for three months and Lydia readily agreed. Knowing the story, the original caregiver looked for another position when the three months were up so that Lydia could continue to work. "I really needed an escape, a place of work where I would have time to think and plan for my life back in Ghana," Lydia said. Three months extended into four months, and before long, Lydia was working full-time. When asked if it was difficult to obtain a work permit, she quickly added: "that too was part of the escape. I was alone with an elderly lady who did not understand me most of the time anyway, so there was limited conversation and no explaining as to the legality of my work status." Lydia worked as an undocumented immigrant. Instead of six months to stay within the legality of her visa, she worked for four years and then decided to go back to Ghana. She explained why she decided to leave the US. "I'm no longer a young woman. I cannot die here and be buried in the snow [laughter]. I am getting to the point where I will soon need care myself; who will do that if I continue to live here? At least if I revive my business, I will be in a better position to care for myself and others in the family the way I used to." In fact, Lydia's case is not atypical. Three other women shared similar stories of entering the US on visitors' visas and ended up overstaying. And although the details of their stories differed, ultimately it was their circumstances coupled with their legal status that made live-in especially attractive for them. The job offered a cover for them to work undetected by law enforcement. What is significant about Lydia's story, and indeed the stories of other women who obtained their jobs in like manner, was the networking and extension of favor by other women in the business. The women seemed to understand the needs of other Ghanaian women and did not withhold information regarding the availability of work from those who needed it. In many cases, women who were already in the system served as reference for their compatriots. Sometimes they trained friends for future positions by using them as proxies.

From a different perspective, Lydia's story speaks to a humanitarian issue that is not seriously addressed in immigration discourse in this country because of the people at the center of the discourse and also the political context in which the discourse occurs. Undocumented immigrants happen to be predominantly people of color most of whom occupy the lowest rung on the economic ladder. When we factor in gender, as in women in domestic service, we have race, class, and gender driving the discourse. We do not try to understand that the thousands of people who want to work in the US, even if illegally, do so because the US symbolizes a final frontier. To many people outside this country, going to the US means going for freedom, security, and prosperity. These are also the issues that limit women's lives in most of the places where immigrant women in this country come from. When they are deported because they are undocumented but not for crimes against the state, they are dealt an injustice that goes against international human rights laws.[42] A report prepared by some NGOs and individuals in the US for the UN Human Rights Committee identified several protective laws that should apply to domestic care workers in this country but are not enforced. Among several parts of the International Covenant on Civil and Political Rights that the report discusses, Articles 7 and 9 help to explain Lydia's story as a humanitarian case. The report states, "Article 7 prohibits cruel, inhuman or degrading treatment while Article 9 guarantees the right to liberty and the security of person."[43] The discourse on undocumented immigrants, even if they are not arrested and deported, occurs in a context that denies women like Lydia the opportunity to freely participate in the economy because of their immigrant status.

Lydia could have gone back to Ghana to face a difficult life in the long term. With nothing to fall back on and only a hope that she might get money through a send-off party that she could not even guarantee would happen, she decided to stay. The decision to stay also raises ethical and moral questions regarding immigrants' options when they become undocumented. Lydia knowingly broke the law and risked being blacklisted by the state. If she was found out she could be removed and then jeopardize her chance of future reentry into the US. If she went back to Ghana she could face an uncertain future. These are tough choices that immigrant women face daily; they are caught in a bind. With no definitive answers to her questions, Lydia was fortunate to secure a job as live-in care worker. The job shielded her from the law while also giving her the opportunity to acquire the capital she needed to restart her business when she went back to Ghana.

Live-in as sanctuary can be understood from another perspective. Usually when we talk about sanctuary in immigration discourse, our attention is immediately drawn to refugees. They are the ones who escape from extreme danger to areas of relative peace and protection. We do not link independent immigrants who are already settled in a destination country with sanctuary. Yet, immigrant women, especially those who were sponsored by spouses, sometimes face marital situations that they deal with in ways that only immigrant women would. In Ghana, people usually resolve marital conflicts through arbitration with church or family elders. A sponsored wife who has not yet established relationships within the immigrant community and is not exposed to the US legal system to utilize it in cases of marital problems will have to find alternative means of resolving her problems. I will use the story of Aminata to illustrate this phenomenon.

Sponsorship remains a major avenue for Ghanaian women who would otherwise not gain admission into the US on their own merit. However, sponsorship sets up a situation for women to be potentially abused by their husbands based on a sense of indebtedness.[44] That, in short, was what happened to Aminata, who was sponsored and joined her husband in 2000. Like many Ghanaian women, Aminata was a trader. She bought foodstuff—plantains, cocoyam, palm nuts, cassava—from her town and surrounding villages and traveled overnight on a large wooden truck to Accra. She would sell the goods and then use the money to buy smoked fish, cosmetics, candles, and other goods for retail in a little shop she ran in her town. By the standards of her community, she was a plain man woman. It was during one of those trips to Accra that she met Allan. He told her about his wonderful life in the US and his desire to share that life with her. They started a relationship. These relationships are quite common in Ghana. Women scramble to befriend borgers in hopes that they would get the chance to travel abroad. Most of the time, though, the relationships end when the men leave. And so Aminata was surprised when her "boyfriend" came back later with the intention of marrying her. Her parents were thrilled that their daughter had made a good choice. The possibility of her traveling to the US meant that the family's material condition could potentially change. As such, Aminata's family did not hesitate to grant the potential son-in-law permission to perform the marital rights.

In the past, that would not have been the case. Aminata is an Akan, and tradition would have required her parents to ask the man to return at a later date for their answer to his request to marry their daughter. That would have given the parents time to investigate the man's background. Were men in his family hardworking? Did they take care of their children? Were they wife beaters? Was there a communicable disease in his family? Had any family member committed a serious crime like murder, incest, robbery? If the woman's parents had concerns in any or some of these issues, they would invite the man back and politely refuse his request. But times have changed. Modernity has changed how certain norms operate. Besides, there was an immediate payoff to the parents if Aminata married Allan who would be required by tradition to give the parents material things, which, in this case, would be goods from the US. These were important considerations as Aminata's parents allowed the marriage to proceed.

In November, 2000, Aminata was ready to join her husband. Reminiscing on the night of her departure, she said, "When I boarded the airplane for the first time, I was full of emotions—anxiety, excitement, happiness and fear (of the flight). I arrived [in the US] and there were lights everywhere at the airport and people were moving very fast and everything looked so beautiful. But it was also very cold." The excitement of arriving in the US quickly fizzled when Aminata realized that a lot of what Allan said about his life were not exactly true. He did not own the apartment he lived in or worked with a bank as he told her and her family in Ghana. He stocked goods in a grocery store. Aminata felt duped but resolved to stay in the marriage. She was in the US, and not even a lying husband would make her go back to Ghana. Whatever Allan's faults, he sponsored her and that meant a lot. This sense of indebtedness to sponsors is a key reason for some immigrant women to stay in abusive relationships. Then also a fight between husband and wife in the US can extend back to Ghana and involve members of each other's families. Some women try to avoid that situation by enduring abuse. Just a week after her arrival Allan told Aminata that he spent a lot of money on her sponsorship and she would have to work to pay off the debt. The good news was that he had found her a job as a janitor. Aminata thought that kind of work was beneath her dignity. She was a hardworking woman; she was doing well in Ghana. What would people say if they heard that she was sweeping in hallways and removing garbage and cleaning toilets? She could do better than a janitor. Aminata was also disappointed that her husband did not allow her time to get to know him. The US seemed very different from what she had heard, but her husband needed his money and there was no time to think about options. She took the janitorial job. She had been in the US for less than two weeks.

Once she started work, Aminata gave her check to her husband every month ending. As a result she could not send her parents any money for quite some time after her arrival in the US. She could only do so if she kept part of her wages. A conversation with her husband turned sour when she asked to know how much her sponsorship cost, how much she had paid, and how much of her wages she could keep as her private money. She had supported her parents before she traveled so her inability to remit them hurt them and humiliated her. The more she talked about money, the angrier her husband became and the harsher his rebuke and insults. Initially Aminata thought that her husband's insults and name-calling were strategies to mask his shame after she found out he lied about his job and living conditions. Besides, she was still getting to know him. They had not stayed together for her to know much about him. But when he beat her the first time, threatened to send her back to Ghana, cut off her friends, and picked her up from her place of work so she would not have the opportunity to interact with other people, Aminata knew she was trapped.

Unknown to Allan, Aminata had used public phones to contact people in the community for help. That was how she got her live-in job. She told her husband that live-in would bring in more money than the janitorial work. Together, they could pool resources and start a project in Ghana. He agreed and she took up the job. During our interview, Aminata explained that she felt the greatest sense of relief when she left home. She found a place of solace where she was free from the constant insults and occasional hitting—a place where she would be free to think deeply about the next stage of her life. For her, live-in was a lifeline. She would stay married but her job would mediate the marriage. She would determine how often she would take days off work and when she did, how long she would stay. Without even thinking about the economic aspect of her job, Aminata could feel the leverage she had in the marriage.

Aminata's story raises two issues that are central to discourse on immigrant live-in care work—isolation and potential or real abuse. When we consider isolation, we do so from the perspective of the employment site, where the worker is the only employee in a house and where she is also the only minority, alien, and poor person. The convergence of race, gender, nationality, and class sharpens the immigrant's sense of isolation and disconnectedness. Similarly, we usually think of the abuse of live-in care workers in relation to their entry status as contract maids and undocumented women whose employers sometimes seize on their special circumstances and do all sorts of horrible things to them. Aminata lived with her husband, but she was very new to the US so that her situation was not very different from a contract maid who had no familial relations and had only her employer(s) to relate to. Aminata exhibited every characteristic of an abused contract maid; the only difference was that a contract maid was at least paid, however small; Aminata lost her wages to her husband because of her sponsored status.

Other married women in the study did not refer to physical abuse as the reason they did live-in. They talked more about their lack of voice and leverage in the family and their belief that if they made enough money, they would be equal partners in their relationships. The women operated on the assumption that money created gender equality in at least one area of their lives—the performance of domestic chores. Much of what they said hinged on gender roles and their husbands' attitudes toward those roles. Two of the women said that prior to working as caregivers they did back-breaking factory work. They were exhausted at the end of the day. Maria, one of them, said that her husband refused to do anything at home because housework was not men's work. Men like Maria's husband believed in a strict gender division of domestic labor but not gender division of the family budget. They expected their wives to contribute, sometimes in equal proportion, to the family budget but they did not want to do any housework. Donkor uncovered a similar trend among married couples in Toronto when she studied the causes of divorce in the Ghanaian community. Women who believed that their husbands should share in domestic chores adopted a policy of "50–50" as a form of protest against their spouses. According to one of those women, she would not do 100% of the housework and then contribute 50% of the family budget.[45] This redefinition of gender roles created tension in some families but it did not lead to the kind of physical or even emotional abuse that Aminata suffered at the hand of her husband. Maria explained that, in Ghana, women live in households with multiple members who share chores and support each other.[46] In the US, the situation is different. Even children want their mothers to serve them. In the end, Maria said, "you feel tired of serving everybody but yourself." For these women, live-in was neither an escape nor a sanctuary. It was not even a protest against men's refusal to perform domestic chores. The talk about house chores was a pretext; the real reason was the potential payoff. As we will see in chapter 5, the women devised ways to take care of their homes while they cared for clients, which indicates that housework was not a big problem in their marriages. The attraction of live-in was the money they hoped to make and the power that money would give them in the family and other areas of social life.

The analysis so far has pointed to a combination of factors that made live-in caregiving attractive to the Ghanaian women. Jobs were available in the personal care sector and they took advantage, based on their personal circumstances and perceptions. They did not believe that racism had something to do with their concentration in that work sector. They understood that the economic situation in Ghana was precarious and that was the reason they immigrated to make their lives and the lives of their dependents better. The practical approach to their expectations as immigrants' versus experts' understanding of domestic care work draws attention to the tenuous relationship between women's agency and experts' view of how that agency is exercised. The fact that the women did not think about their work in relation to racism did not mean that race had nothing to do with the concentration of women of color in domestic care work. The women simply refused to be constrained by it.

We should also note that live-in offered the women the liquid cash they needed. Several of them indicated that they would want to start their own businesses when they went back to Ghana in the future. Four of the women had already built houses in Ghana and needed seed money to start a trade. Others were at different stages of completing their houses or had acquired plots of land to start building. Since they had lived abroad for longer periods and changed their nationalities, they were not certain that they would be able to secure government loans. Having their own money eliminated that uncertainty. Homeownership was also very important because houses served as status symbol and a permanent reminder that the owner was a borger. Owning a house in one's community also grounded one as a bona fide member of that community regardless of one's legal status in the immigrant-receiving country. Importantly, home ownership could serve as old-age security. Instead of working well into their old age, a homeowner could rent out rooms and generate income for their upkeep. These were very important considerations for the immigrant women. Beyond using care work as a pathway to a less stressful future, the women believed that the money they brought home would make them equal power brokers in the family. Whether or not that happened is a different story.

NOTES

1. *Women in America: Indicators of Social and Economic Well-Being,* U.S. Department of Commerce, Economics and Statistics Administration and the Executive Office of the President, Office of Management and Budget, for the White House Council on Women and Girls, March 2011, 35.

2. Tera W. Hunter, "Domination and Resistance: The Politics of Wage Household Labor in New South Atlanta," in *We Specialize in the Wholly Impossible: A Reader in Black Women's History*, ed. Darlene Clark Hine, Wilma Kin and Linda Reed (Brooklyn, NY: Carlson Publishing, Inc., 1995), 344; Paula Giddings, *When and Where I*

Enter: The Impact of Black Women on Race and Sex in America (New York: Bantam Boks, 1984), 48.

3. See Linda Martin and Kerry Segrave, *The Servant Problem: Domestics Workers in North America* (Jefferson, N. C.: McFarland, 1985); Colwin M. Wilson and Leon C. Wilson, "Domestic Work in the United States of America: Past Perspectives and Future Directions," n.d., http://www.rcgd.isr.umich.edu/prba/perspectives/winter2000/cwilson.pdf.

4. Linda Brent, "Incidents in the Life of a Slave Girl," in *The Classic Slave Narratives,* ed. Henry Louis Gates, Jr. (New York: New American Library, 1987), 366–8.

5. Vanessa H. May, *Unprotected Labor: Household Workers, Politics and Middle Class Reform in New York, 1870–1840* (Chapel Hill, NC: University of North Carolina Press, 2011), 17–18.

6. Rebecca Sharpless, *Cooking in Other Women's Kitchens: Domestic Workers in the South, 1865–1960* (Chapel Hill, NC: University of North Carolina Press, 2010), 66.

7. Sharpless, *Cooking in Other Women's Kitchens,* 66.

8. Sharpless, *Cooking in Other Women's Kitchens,* 74.

9. Sharpless, *Cooking in Other Women's Kitchens,* 74.

10. Sharpless, *Cooking in Other Women's Kitchens,* 89; May, *Unprotected Labor,* 8.

11. See Human Rights Watch, "Hidden in the Home: Abuse of Domestic Workers with Special Visas in the United States," Vol 13, no. 2 (G), (June 2001): 5.

12. Human Rights Watch, "Hidden in the Home," 4.

13. Human Rights Watch, "Hidden in the Home," 4.

14. Ehrenreich and Hochschild, "Introduction," 3–5.

15. Ehrenreich and Hochschild, "Introduction," 3.

16. Ehrenreich and Hochschild, "Introduction," 3.

17. The Centers for Disease Control and Prevention reported that life expectancy in the US in 2014 was 78.8 years, while the crude death rate for blacks and whites decreased consistently from 1960–2014. For more details, see Kenneth D. Kochanek, Sherry L. Murphy, Jiaquan Xu and Betzaida Tejada-Vera, "Deaths: Final Data for 2014," *National Vital Statistics Report* 65, no.4, June 30, 2016, 3–6, https://www.cdc.gov/nchs/fastats/life-expectancy.htm.

18. A CNBC report projects a rather gloomy outlook for Americans in the next twenty years. The report cites a study conducted in the UK that projects that the US will experience the lowest life expectancy rates of all the industrialized nations by 2030. Even so, the study predicts that US life expectancy rates will be 83.3 years for women and 79.5 years for men, an appreciation from the current rates of 81.2 years for women and 76.5 years for men. Seen from this angle, it is still possible to expect a spike in the senior population in the next twenty years. See Sam Meredith, "US Life Expectancy is Low and is now Projected to be on Par with Mexico by 2030," Wednesday, February 22, 2017, http://www.cnbc.com/2017/02/22/us-life-expectancy-is-low-and-is-now-projected-to-be-on-par-with-mexico-by-2030.html.

19. CBS News, "Growing Old, Baby Boomer Style," January 10, 2006, http://www.cbsnews.com/news/growing-old-baby-boomer-style.

20. Debra Auerbach, "Best bets for jobs in 2012," January 2, 2012, http://www.CareerBuilder.com.

21. Ehrenreich and Hochschild, "Introduction," 3.

22. *Women in America*, 19.

23. *Women in America: Indicators of Social and Economic Well-Being,* U.S. Department of Commerce, Economics and Statistics Administration and the Executive Office of the President, Office of Management and Budget, for the White House Council on Women and Girls, March 2011, 27.

24. Mark Greenberg, "New Steps for Federal Child Care Policy," *The Future of Children* 17, no. 2 (Fall 2007): 74.

25. H.W. Brands et al., *American Stories: A History of the United States*, (Upper Saddle River, NJ: Pearson, 2015), 739.

26. H.W. Brands et al., *American Stories*, 757.

27. Donkor, "Education of Immigrant Women," 117–120.

28. Goran Hyden, *Beyond Ujamaa in Tanzania: Underdevelopment and an Uncaptured Peasantry* (Berkeley: University of California Press 1980), 8.

29. Tony Waters "A Cultural Analysis of the Economy of Affection and the Uncaptured Peasantry in Tanzania," *Journal of Modern African Studies* 30, no. 1 (March 1992): 166.

30. As I was writing this chapter, an article appeared in the Ghanaian media that praised a former president for finally building a house in his hometown. Apparently his townsfolk had criticized him for not doing so for a long time. For full details, see "Former President Mahama builds multi-million cedi mansion in Bole," ghanaweb, May 19, 2017, www.ghanaweb.com.

31. A billionaire politician in Ghana, Kennedy Ohene Agyapong, perfectly exemplifies this phenomenon. He lived in several places in Europe and then settled in the US before relocating to Ghana. He has developed his village into a modern 'first world' enclave and explains why and how he did it. See the documentary at "Autograph on Joy Prime: Nathaniel Attoh interviews Hon. Kennedy Agyapong," https://www.youtube.com/watch?v=JlMKjGsf2P8.

32. The *Huffington Post* carried the story of a Ghanaian immigrant in Canada who was installed chief of his town but, instead of staying on to rule, returned to Canada and continued working as a landscaper. At the same time, he and his boss formed a foundation that collects items to ship to Ghana to help his subjects. For the full story, see Elyse Wanshel, "Landscaper in Canada become King in Ghana, Still Mows Lawns," *Huffington Post,* September 29, 2016, http://www.huffingtonpost.com/entry/eric-manu-west-african-tribe-king-landscaper-canada-healthcare_us_57e153a1e4b04a1497b6ba2b; see also Valentina Mazzucato, "The Double Engagement: Transnationalism and Integration. Ghanaian Migrants' Lives between Ghana and the Netherlands," *Journal of Ethnic and Migration Studies* 34, no. 2 (March 2008): 203; Panapress "Ghanaians abroad send back home up to a billion," http://www.panapress.com/Ghanaians-abroad-send-back-home-up-to-a-billion-dollars--12-554915-72-lang4-index.html.

33. During a trip I made to Ghana in summer 2016, my mother complained that I had not built a house in our town. Her argument was that she will be respected, glorified even, if I build a house. And so now the pressure is on me to oblige, particularly in light of her age.

34. A. B. K. Kasozi, *The Integration of Black African Immigrants in Canadian Society: A Case Study of Toronto CMA* (Toronto: Canadian African Newcomer Aid Centre of Toronto: 1986), 1–2; see also Edward Opoku-Dapaah, *Adaptation of Ghanaian Refugees in Toronto*, (North York: York Lanes Press, 1993), 7–8.

35. Ghanaian immigrant women in Canada adopted that approach toward their job prospects. They went back to school and changed their jobs from factory work to white-collar jobs. See Donkor, "The Education of Immigrant Women," 117–147.

36. Anita Ilta Garey and Karen V. Hansen, eds., *At the Heart of Work and Family: Engaging the Ideas of Arlie Hochschild* (New Jersey: Rutgers University Press, 2015), 19.

37. Philomena Essed, *Diversity: Gender, Colour and Culture* (Amherst: University of Massachusetts Press, 1996), 59–60.

38. Martha Donkor, "Looking Back and Looking In," *journal of International Migration and Integration* 5, no. 1 (Winter 2004): 45–7.

39. Unless otherwise stated, all names used in the narratives throughout the book are pseudonyms to protect the identity of the participants.

40. The other women on visitors' visas were gainfully employed but wanted to start their own businesses so they came to the US to do live-in; they usually replaced people who were traveling. Generally, these women work for short periods and then return to Ghana. They will do this until they have met their target; then they may stop coming to the US or will visit but not do live-in. These transient workers have popularized caregiving among their colleagues and friends in Ghana.

41. Chandra Talpade Mohanty, "Under Western Eyes: Feminist Scholarship and Colonial Discourses," *Boundary 2*, 12, no. 3, (Spring-Autumn, 1984): 335–8.

42. "Domestic Workers Rights in the United States," http://www.law.unc.edu/documents/clinicalprograms/domesticworkersreport.pdf.

43. Quoted in "Domestic Workers Rights in the United States."

44. Martha Donkor, "I'm Divorcing because I Drank Lake Ontario: Marital Breakdown in Ghanaian Immigrant Families in Toronto," *Southern Journal of Canadian Studies* 5, nos. 1–2 (December 2012): 252.

45. Donkor, "I'm Divorcing because I Drank Lake Ontario," 251.

46. Maria's description of households full of women needs clarification. Women who migrate from one area to another as a result of work or marriage will not have the benefit of the support of other women. Maria's claim is also an exaggeration because in households of multiple women, each woman organizes her kitchen separately. Women may rely on children to perform house chores or they may be solely responsible.

Chapter 5

The Dynamics of Live-in Caregiving

Live-in caregiving has a long record in our nation's history. It has been performed by women of different races and ethnicities at different times; however, certain characteristics of the job have persisted regardless of who did it and when. Scholars and other experts have identified problems of isolation, abuse, undervaluation, and exploitation that women suffer in the performance of their work as caregivers. However, women in private practice appeared to have different perceptions of these problems, even though they acknowledged that the problems existed. Thus it is important to examine how the women performed their job, their relationships with their employers, wages, and other aspects of work in an attempt to understand their responses in situations of abuse, isolation, and exploitation and undervaluation that made them have different perceptions of those problems.

It is obvious to the casual observer that isolation, abuse, and exploitation work in tandem. As an illustration, imagine a thirty-year-old woman with limited facility in English, who has never traveled outside her country, has been recruited on contract to work for an upper-class white American family. She responded to an advertisement posted by a recruitment agency that painted a glowing picture of work and life in the US. She had hopes of improving her life and the lives of other members of her family. She left her country the previous day and arrived in the US nearly fourteen hours later. A fifty-year-old white woman, one of four people she will be living with, picks her up at the airport. There is small talk as they drive home. The house is big, modern, beautiful, and isolated from other houses in the neighborhood. Before she is shown her room, two young boys are introduced to her as the children. She is taken to her living space in the basement, and then comes up again for some food and "orientation." She starts work the very next morning as general house help. This means she will clean, cook, do the laundry, do the dishes, make beds, take the children out to play, etc. This worker does not get time to experience jet lag or walk through the neighborhood to familiarize herself with her surroundings.

This scenario actually describes the reality of many live-in domestic workers, on contract or not. They experience a deep sense of loneliness and alienation and sometimes hunger because they may not be used to eating American foods. A direct outcome of the isolation of domestic caregivers is their invisibility, a condition that makes them vulnerable to abuse and financial exploitation because they are governed by labor laws of the US that are not generally enforced.[1] The abuse of immigrant domestic workers is not an American problem. It is a global problem that has been extensively researched and disseminated. In the US, Asia, and Middle Eastern countries, where live-in caregivers mostly have their jobs, there have been reports of extreme abuse including hitting, sleeping in dark, dingy rooms, starvation, withholding of wages, restriction of movement, sexual harassment, and other treatments that together seem like a form of slavery.[2] Filipina and Indonesian maids appear to be the most vulnerable in these phenomena in Asian and Middle Eastern countries. For instance, the *Kuwait Times* carried the story of a housemaid who was maltreated by her employers to the extent that she was permanently disabled:

> The case file indicated the victim had been working for the second suspect and his wife (first suspect) since 2011, alleging the first suspect consistently maltreated her for three years to the point of torturing her with pressing iron, iron rod and cable in different parts of the body. The plaintiff claimed the couple restrained her from leaving the house to prevent her from lodging a complaint against them. Later, she managed to escape from the house to lodge a complaint supported by a medical report that showed burns, fractures and bruises all over her body.[3]

Sometimes maids were not lucky when they attempted to escape from their employers. A Filipina maid in Kuwait fell from a fourth floor window while attempting to escape by using a bedsheet to climb down a window. The sheet snapped and she fell to her death.[4] Other times the women fell from high-rises when their employers asked them to clean windows without harnesses to hold them in place. Such was the case in Serangoon, Singapore, in May 2012, when an Indonesian domestic worker fell from a high-rise to her death. Bridget Tan, president of Humanitarian Organization for Migration Economics, revealed that the incident was the ninth such death of the year in Serangoon alone.[5]

These are bizarre deaths that have not been reported in the US. However, it will be a mistake to assume that live-in caregivers in the US do not suffer abuse because they are not falling out of windows to their death. The Human Rights Watch has systematically collected stories from women who experienced horrible treatment at the hands of their employers in the US. Included in their accounts are women who suffered from assault and battery, restrictions on movement, confiscation of travel documents, threat of deportation, and long workdays.[6] Ehrenreich and Hochschild's edited volume, *Global Woman*, contains stories of care workers from different countries who suffered different kinds of indignities.[7] One of the cruelest cases of abuse that reached the US First Circuit Court is *US v. Alzanki*, 1995. The defendant, Talal Alzanki, was a Kuwaiti student who lived in Quincy, Massachusetts, with his wife; the victim was a Sri Lankan woman who had worked for the Alzanki family in Kuwait before she was sent to the US in 1992 to work for the couple who had a special needs child. Upon arrival the Alzankis seized her passport, forbad her to step out of the house, overworked her, hit her, and starved her. She was able to escape and report her case to the authorities only when a nurse visited the house while the couple was not at home.[8] Other care workers have reported sexual harassment, threat of deportation, and being overworked.[9]

Apart from harm to their physical bodies, immigrant domestic workers have been under-remunerated. A Singaporean domestic worker who ingested rat poison in an apparent suicide attempt told police that she had worked for seven months and had earned the equivalent of US$53.[10] In the US, researchers and labor activists have decried the appallingly low wages that employers pay domestic workers. For instance, the University of North Carolina School of Law Human Rights Policy Clinic in conjunction with several non-governmental organizations and individuals issued a report to the United Nations Human Rights Committee that emphasized, among other forms of abuse, that domestic workers received wages that were below the minimum wage.[11] The abuse of immigrant domestic care workers is a global issue; wherever immigrant women take up domestic care work, we can be sure of abuse.

A closer examination of the abuse that immigrant domestic workers suffer shows, on the surface, that a lot of it is not different from other forms of domestic violence that occur in homes across the country and hidden from the public gaze. For instance, a Washington, D.C., couple was convicted of manslaughter in 2013 for the death of their adopted thirteen-year-old daughter. The prosecutor in the case told a news outlet that the girl slept in a closet, was not allowed to use the toilet facilities in the main house, and was fed cold and frozen foods. Her emaciated dead body was found at the back of the couple's house.[12] While the details differ, the death of the US child and that of the Filipino woman in Singapore share the common element of having occurred under a cloud of domestic secrecy where the victims lacked power. What differentiates the violence that immigrant domestic workers suffer from that of American citizens is the power dynamic defined by race, class, and "immigrantness." Immigrant women are degraded in ways that mostly happen to children with no power or agency in the family setting. It is this infantilization of domestic workers that makes their abuse that much harder to take. Whether in Asian countries or in the US, the stories of abuse outlined above occurred to immigrant women who had entered into legal contracts with the families that sponsored them. The women's misunderstanding of the legal implications of their contract and problems of language coupled with their isolation greatly increased their susceptibility to abuse. The same was true of undocumented women who would not report abuse for fear that they would be repatriated.[13] Given these empirical cases of abuse, it will be interesting to find out how the Ghanaian women responded to their employers in a type of care work that the women deemed to be superior to others.

GHANAIAN WOMEN IN PRIVATE PRACTICE

Unlike women who enter the US with special visas to work for particular families or individuals, the Ghanaian women arrived without any such contracts. Those who lived in Europe via Nigeria had learned lessons in immigrant adaptation and were more likely to know how to navigate their way in the American labor market. Others arrived as legally sponsored immigrants by husbands who were already settled; this group of women would have help in the initial settlement process, including looking for a job. Those who arrived on their own as independent immigrants or asylees had the benefit of a young Ghanaian immigrant community in New York City, where they could network within the churches, ethnic and town associations. These initial circumstances were important in determining the women's attitudes toward work. Women who were sponsored by their husbands would be under immediate pressure to find work while those who were not sponsored had the benefit of networking for jobs within the various churches and associations. It is not surprising that when they decided to go into live-in caregiving, the women chose to work with mostly middle upper-class white men who lived alone. Almost all the women had previously worked as live-out caregivers through agencies that recruited people for these jobs. The experiences the women gained working as live-out helped them to decide who they wanted to work with and in what form.

The women's boldness in this manner stemmed from the fact that they were already settled in the US and knew their way around. They could go back to other forms of employment if their current arrangements did not work.[4] It is also noteworthy that the women appeared to have preferences in clients based on gender. Only three of the twenty-six women who participated in the study took care of women. Two women took care of men whose wives lived at home but were not clients. All other clients were men, in their late seventies or older. A few had health issues that required extra attention. In most cases, the relationships that the women forged at their places of work were relationships that began long before the women moved in with their clients. The women's choice of men instead of women to care for was also revealing. One woman said pointedly that she would not work for a woman as long as there were men to work for because, according to her, female clients were difficult to work for. Another woman said that women were more likely than men to yell or say hurtful things to workers. A third woman disagreed, saying that female clients had done housework at some point in their lives. Therefore they would be able to tell readily if a worker was doing her work right or not. These differing opinions about preferring male to female clients speaks to the difficulty, and perhaps even the danger, of making generalizations about a work sector where a person's experience is often mediated by temperament. Even so, it is important to point out that there appears to be a woman-to-woman dynamic in domestic work that reveals how race and class sets up hierarchies and tension among differently situated women.

The women characterized their work as "private practice," (sometimes as private service) to differentiate it as well as raise its status from other forms of domestic work. From their perspective, private practice was the "one percent" of home care work. This is particularly interesting in light of the image that the public has of paid domestic work generally as low class and low value work. Obviously the women were not concerned about public perceptions of their work; their focus was on how they compared to other domestic care workers. Theirs was high class because they did not care for people who were too needy or totally dependent. They did not have to deal with people who would scrutinize every move they made. Thus when they called their type of care work as private practice they were reflecting the true character of their job. "Private Practice," as some of us might recall, was the name of a popular television medical drama series. It is not clear whether or not the Ghanaian women knew about the series and decided to name their work after it for prestige. Interestingly, there appears to be a commonality between the television drama and the women's work in three aspects—the act of moving from home to a new work area, the fact of self-employment, and care as the focus of work. Just to give one example, in *Private Practice*, the drama, Dr. Addison Forbes Montgomery made a personal decision to move from Seattle to Santa Monica to join a group of doctors;[15] in private practice, the women's work, they made individual decisions to shift from live-out to live-in, which necessitated moving from home to a work site. Beyond that, there was little, if any, to compare the women's work with the television series. The women's work was real, the series was only entertainment, not real. However, the fact that the women named their type of care work after a highly rated television series meant that they had owned it and took pride in it.

Another feature that was unique with private practice was that the women did not obtain their jobs through an employment agency. Almost all the women had worked through employment agencies at points in their work history. In fact, most of them were introduced to their employers as live-out caregivers by employment agencies. As they worked, they gained a deeper understanding of how care work must proceed. They could not reconcile the idea that they were on the frontlines doing the heavy lifting to the fact that the employment agencies paid them a small fraction of the money they believed clients paid to the agencies. One woman explained that she made $7:25 an hour as a live-out caregiver without any employment benefits. So she started private conversations with her employer, asking him what it would take for him to have her work for him full-time but cutting out the employment agency. Thus they bypassed the employment agencies and negotiated the terms of their employment. From this humble beginning, private practice took off in the Ghanaian community. Yet, unlike other forms of home care, private practice employs a relatively small number of workers. Its characteristics offer perspectives on live-in care work that do not always accord with the standard views of abuse, exploitation, and undervaluation that have characterized much of the literature of other forms of domestic care work.

Of all the areas of concern that scholars have identified with home care work, invisibility seems to be the common element that links private practice with other types of care work. Invisibility as used here goes beyond its literal meaning. It means the lack of recognition of private practice as a separate component of domestic care work due to the workers' inability to organize as a unit.[16] Domestic workers in some areas can organize to demand better conditions of work because they can identify a single employer and patterns in their conditions of work although they are excluded from certain aspects of the Fair Labor Standards Act.[17] Not so with private practice. Women may know each other from the immigrant community but they would not necessarily know the work conditions of others to make comparisons and hence organize as a group to ask for better conditions of service. In the sections that follow, I use vignettes to probe issues of isolation, abuse, exploitation/under-remuneration, and undervaluation in private practice.

The Problem of Abuse: Nancy and Elsie

Nancy had been a live-in caregiver for sixteen years. She was taking care of her third client at the time of our interview. She said that there was no uniformity in the work conditions in private service. How a woman experienced her job depended very much on the temperament of the employer and tolerance of the employee. She recalled working for an eighty-two-year-old man who was curious about foreign cultures. Nancy capitalized on that and introduced him to some Ghanaian dishes. They also watched Akan drama (drama in a local Ghanaian language), which she explained to him in English. On a few occasions she took him to a Ghanaian church service. Nancy said that she had her best experience of caregiving working for that man. She spoke with nostalgia about the times that they would watch a Ghanaian drama and then she would explain the larger context for some of the plots in her broken English that made the man laugh. But then Nancy explained that he understood her and they got on well. Five years into her employment with him, the man had a heart attack and died. Asked how it was that they seemed to have the kind of synergy that she described, Nancy said that she did what she was supposed to do. In other words, she met the expectations of her employer by being robotic. She cooked, cleaned, did the laundry, and accompanied him to appointments, restaurants, and amusement places. She noted that the man was old and had health issues and the least she could do was to make the rest of his life comfortable. But then she made a comment that was remarkable. Nancy indicated that the man had a lot of money. How did she even know that her employer had a lot of money? Did she have access to his bank account? Did she work to please him in hopes that he might leave her some of his money upon his death? Nancy did not provide direct answers to these questions, other than explaining that some employers go out of their way to give things to dedicated and faithful employees. Her employer had given her things other than her regular wages, which perhaps explained her dedication to him. It does appear that Nancy got close enough to her employer to gain his confidence and possibly access to his purse.[18]

Nancy's work experience contrasted sharply with Elsie's. Elsie took care of an elderly gentleman in his late seventies who, like Nancy's client, also lived alone. However, in terms of job description and relationship with her employer, Elsie's experience was very different from Nancy's. Elsie said that she performed "light service"—prepared breakfast daily, did laundry, and gave him bed baths when he was quite ill. Her employer's children often stopped by to drop off food, which relieved her of that chore on most days. It was on the personal level that Elsie found her work quite challenging. She did not have the kind of friendly, personal relationship with her employer that could minimize the boredom she experienced. Conversations between them were mostly terse and sometimes even cold. Importantly, Elsie did not like that she slept in a small, poorly ventilated room in the basement. She said, "My isolation in the basement makes me feel like a person with a communicable disease who has to be quarantined from the rest of the household. I don't understand why his children will make this arrangement, knowing that I cook for him every day. If I have a disease, I guess I can infect him by cooking his food..." The disease analogy was remarkable in the sense that Elsie did not consider how her living arrangement could affect her own health but instead griped over a condition that was nonexistent.

Elsie's sleeping arrangement was not her only issue. She explained that given her client's health condition, there were times she had to help him at night with his medications or call emergency services to examine him. In these situations, her client called out to her and she had to rush from the basement to the main floor to take care of him. She could make several trips up the stairs in one night when he was not feeling well. She observed, "I'm afraid that one of these days he will call and I will not hear. I sleep when I go to bed, you know. So if he calls and I don't hear and something happens to him, who should be blamed? I hope it doesn't happen but if it does, I guess his children will blame themselves for putting me in the basement." Elsie's shift of blame was interesting in two ways. First, she seemed to suggest that but for his children, the elderly gentleman would be fine with her at a level that would make her feel wanted and appreciated. Second, she did not realize that her accommodation in the basement held symbolic meaning. It represented a physical separation based on race, gender, and class. She was black, a woman, and an employee while the client and his family were white, men, and high society employers. But did this separation necessarily mean that Elsie was abused and Nancy was not? In fact, most people who have worked in certain kinds of factories might identify with Elsie in terms of the separation of physical space between employer(s) and employees.[19] If Elsie escaped the impact of capitalist globalization in Ghana, she certainly experienced it first hand in the US in a different form. It may well have been that the employer and his children did not even consider Elsie as a worker but rather a helper who had to be compensated to keep on helping for as long as the family needed help. While it is only a conjecture, it smells of infantilization.

It is obvious that Nancy and Elsie represented opposite ends of the range of relationships that women cultivated with their employers. Most women in private practice had tolerable relations with their clients. They did not experience the kinds of physical abuse that other domestic workers have reported experiencing perhaps because in almost all cases, the women lived alone with their employers who happened to be quite old and in certain cases frail. The clients would not be in a position to physically harm the women even if they had the propensity to do so. The women also exhibited a degree of self-assurance because they had options. They could move out and find other employment if their clients attempted to abuse them. Their self-assurance also rested on the fact that with the exception of the four on visitors' visas, the remaining were legal immigrants, some naturalized and others on their way to naturalization. Even so, there were nuances of abusive behavior on the part of clients that were so subtle that one had to peel the surface to reveal the abuse for what it was. One of these related to time off for the women. There was not uniformity in the number and frequency of time women could take off work. Different employers had different arrangements with their workers. One woman, twenty-four years, single, and no children, said that she got days off every four months. Another woman, on a visitor's visa, said she worked for six straight months without taking time off. By and large, women and their clients worked out convenient schedules that were mutually agreeable. Problems arose, however, when an emergency occurred and women had to go home when it was not yet time for their days off. Employers would usually place their needs above the women's needs and would be reluctant to grant women leave, even though women were not paid on their days off. That precisely was the problem Akua faced when she had to respond to an emergency.

Akua had been taking care of a seventy-nine-year-old man. She said that relations between them were strictly business-like. Her employer spoke to her only when it was necessary to say something; and while she liked that arrangement, there was always a level of trepidation when she had to ask him a question. Asked why she would choose to work with a person with whom she did not have a rapport, Akua said that she selected him because he was naturally quiet; she did not think that he would change into the cold, withdrawn person he became. The emergent situation that Akua had to attend to involved her ex-husband, the man who sponsored her immigration into the US and with whom she had three children. The man passed away suddenly and although it was not yet her time off, Akua had to go home. Here is part of the conversation that Akua said took place between her and her employer regarding her request to go home:

Akua: "I need some days off; someone died."
Employer: "Who died?"
Akua: "My ex-husband."
Employer: "Oh, I'm sorry to hear that. But what are you going home for?"
Akua: "I have to be there."
Employer: "Why? The man was your ex! Did he have a wife?"
Akua: "He was married but I'm not going there because of his wife."
Employer: "If he is the reason you must go home and he is dead, what is your argument?"
Akua: "I'm not arguing; I'm telling you that I must go home…"

Akua's verbal exchange with her employer resembles similar incidents reported by Pierrette Hondagneu-Sotelo. In her study, the women stood up to their employers when necessary while others employed low key but effective tactics to make their case.[20] Unlike one of Hondagneu-Sotelo's subjects who stood up to be employer when she had already made up her mind of quitting her job, Akua did not intend to quit. She was rather bewildered by the back-and-forth. Her children, all underage, lived with their father and stepmother. She should be home to comfort them and make new living arrangements in case their stepmother decided not to continue living with them (which was more likely going to be the case). Also, she had to know if the deceased's family in Ghana would ask for the body to be flown home and what her children's decisions would be in that regard. If the children decided that they would go to Ghana with the body (assuming that was what was going to happen), then she would have to go with them. These were important and private issues that had to be hashed out in person and not from a distance over the phone. She was thus frustrated that her employer would even try to stand in her way when he did not understand Akan culture. Ultimately Akua defied her employer and took some days off, but she called in a proxy so that her employer would not be alone.[21]

Another woman corroborated Akua's story by indicating that her employer did not want to give her time off to attend a social event because he did not see any important role that she would play at the function. She too, defied the employer. By every measure these were abusive situations because they were attempts to restrict the women's movement. However, the women thought that such situations only revealed the vulnerability and dependence of their clients. The fact that they defied their employers and continued working for them without being fired was remarkable. The women had an understanding of their own self-worth or at least an understanding of their responsibilities outside of work. It is this self-assurance that distinguished women in private practice from other forms of domestic care.

Central to Akua's story is what I term the cultural disconnect. Both parties, Akua and her client, did not understand certain aspects of each other's culture. The white employer did not understand the role that an ex-spouse could play in such a situation. He did not understand that the spouse of a deceased person (certainly among the Akan) could not make unilateral decisions regarding the death of the spouse. The maternal family of the deceased in Ghana might make very important calls like where the body would be buried, when, and the quality of coffin to bury him in, etc. However, the family would expect the spouse living in the US to bear the greater part, if not all, of the financial burden. The fact that Akua had children by the deceased put her squarely in the deliberations to the extent that the decisions affected her children. If the children were adults in Ghana, they would have been expected to buy the coffin even though their father would have been married. That was the tradition. On the other hand, Akua did not understand that death in American culture is not celebrated as elaborately and with as much ritual as happens among the Akan in Ghana. In most situations, people are buried within a week of death in the US. Among the Akan, the earliest that a person may be buried these days is within six weeks of death. And while waiting for the burial and funeral and church service if the person was a Christian, there would be a one-week celebration. Akua would be expected to participate in all these rituals even though she was divorced from the man.

The cultural disconnect certainly frustrated and annoyed both of them, but it did not lead to the severance of the work relationship. The process of becoming live-in caregivers in private practice established an initial element of knowledge of each other's temperament that allowed for the frank exchange of ideas even when both sides did not agree. And while the potential for abuse was always present in these kinds of situations, the rapport that women established with their employers greatly reduced the possibility of abuse occurring. The point is that it takes a certain level of trust for two people from culturally, socially, and economically different backgrounds to enter into an exclusive, private agreement to care for and to receive care. And given that the employers were sometimes needy and also older, the potential for abuse could easily turn against them if the women were so inclined. That has happened in a number of cases in other contexts.

Some of us were shocked when news broke in late March 2017 that an elderly woman in an assisted living facility in Missouri had been raped.[22] It just so happened that the rape of seniors at certain facilities in the country has been a long-standing serious problem. Chris Serres of the *Star Tribune* reported that in 2013, a thirty-year-old worker at a facility in Edgewood Vista in Hermantown, Minnesota, raped an 89-year-old woman.[23] Serres went on to write that other forms of physical abuse including slapping, pinching, and taunting had occurred at the facility.[24] There have also been several stories of live-in caregivers stealing money from their clients. For instance, a 23-year-old Missouri caregiver spent $3,500 on her client's debit card,[25] while a 41-year-old woman from Louisville, Kentucky, pawned jewelry she stole from her 88-year-old client for $10,000.[26] The rapist and the fraudulent duo were native-born white Americans. Could it be that immigrant caregivers would not abuse their clients because of their immigrant status? The evidence suggests otherwise, although in my own research I did not uncover cases of theft by any of the women who participated in the study. The women rather had interesting stories to tell concerning the financial abuse of elderly clients by other care workers. They had heard that some people abuse seniors, especially in assisted facilities but not in private practice where most clients were relatively stronger and did not need the kind of help that seniors in assisted homes require. None of the women said that they had ever abused their clients. Instead, they appealed to their cultural background and traditions surrounding old age and explained that old age was revered and sometimes even celebrated. It would be culturally inappropriate to abuse an elderly person simply because they were in positions to do so. Yet, that view was contradicted by an incident that was reported in the *Times Ledger* in 2012. A 53-year-old Ghanaian live-in caregiver cared for an 86-year-old widowed, wheelchair bound woman in New York. The client not only paid the caregiver $81,000 a year (which was highly suspect); she also allowed the caregiver's two young children to move in with them, another unusual step in live-in caregiving arrangements.[27] By all appearances employer and employee had become a family. The old lady trusted the caregiver to such an extent that she allowed the caregiver to write checks for the family's expenses. Somehow, over a period of four years, from 2007 to 2011, the caregiver wrote checks to herself to the tune of $791,054.[28]

The potential for the abuse of care recipients in private practice was particularly high. By and large, there were only two people, caregiver and care receiver, one relatively younger and stronger and the other older and sometimes frail, living alone. The women did not have to engage in physically aggressive behavior toward their clients. Take Elsie, for example. If she pretended to be asleep and not respond to her employer's nighttime calls, something bad could have happened to him. Akua could have starved her employer by not preparing food for him when she defied him and took days off. Other subtle means of abuse could include taking things and money. The fact that the women did not do so speaks to their sense of decency as individuals. It is not certain whether or not the women knew about the theft case described above; however, their view of workers who abused their clients was one of disdain. Nancy indicated that it would be foolhardiness to build a strong relationship with a client and then ruin it by stealing from him. She would be outraged and perhaps walk out on her employer if he abused her; in the same way, she believed her client would not like it if she abused him. Nancy's rationalization made sense when viewed against the backdrop of the difficulty involved in working one's way toward securing a private practice position. Once secured, both parties understood that they needed each other. The women seemed to like their work while the employers depended on the women for their well-being. This symbiosis ensured that for the most part, employers and employees lived together in harmony. In short, the potential for abuse or actual abuse that has dominated discourse on domestic work did not appear to be a central issue of concern for the Ghanaian women in private practice because they did not experience the kinds of blatant abuse that have been recorded in other studies. It is also evident that abuse or potential abuse did not work in one direction.

Undervaluation of Paid Domestic Work

There is no doubt that the American public does not attach a high value to paid domestic work. That view has roots in the extreme racism that characterized the lives African American women who dominated domestic work. There is also the notion in the popular consciousness that the value of work is linked to its monetary compensation. And since the low wages that African American women were paid continued to characterize domestic work long after they ceased to dominate that sector, the perception has followed paid domestic work to the present. What has been given short shrift in the analysis is asking the people at the center—the care workers—about the value *they* attach to their work. It must mean something for women to be employed as care workers. Some women in Hondagneu-Sotelo's study expressed sadness when they had to walk away from children they had cared for and bonded with.[29] Nancy, in this study, spoke with nostalgia about a client she cared for. These cases reveal the affection and sensitivity that the care workers had for the individuals they cared for. Now affection and sensitivity lead to the larger question of value. Of course asking people in a particular job sector to place a value on their work may sound rhetorical especially if they are aware of public perceptions of the job. Some may be apologetic in order to hide the flaws in their area of work. However, we can follow Clare Ungerson's lead and emphasize that the value of care work must not necessarily lie in its monetary compensation alone.[30] The value must also lie in the satisfaction that the caregiver derives in the knowledge that she has been able to make another person's life worthwhile. The Ghanaian women emphasized the qualitative and spiritual satisfaction they derived by offering private care. I will use an incident that occurred in January 2015 to elucidate. A Ghanaian politician was alleged to have made derogatory comments about immigrants engaged in domestic care work. In a scathing response to the alleged insult, a group of women in Chicago issued a strong retort:

> if he [the politician] was aiming directly at care givers, he should know that those hardworking men and women are engaged in one of the most honorable occupations ever. The system makes it possible for these compassionate individuals to take good care of old, disabled, or mentally challenged people who would otherwise have a hard time taking care of themselves. Ghana would be heaven if we had a whole industry dedicated to helping and taking care of such people.[31]

The comment reflected the views of the women who participated in this study. They did not see any shame in doing domestic work. Badu, one of the women, said that live-in caregiving was certainly not a Silicon Valley job, but it was honest labor that generated a decent income apart from the satisfaction that it makes other people's lives better. As she explained, "I would have loved to dress up in the morning and drive to work in a nice office among professionals. I did not get to do that kind of job but I can tell you one thing: whether in a plush office or someone else's home, we all satisfy a need and bring money home at the end of the month. I have not heard that a woman wasn't paid because she did care work." Badu also observed that if Americans stigmatize domestic work, then it is their problem. That positive attitude toward their work was important in sustaining their interest in the work. Their attitude recalls an Akan adage that literally translates "I care for you to teethe; you care for me to shed mine." This proverb is used by close family members to express the expectation that their investment in younger members of the family should be considered as a form of old-age security. In other words, younger family members must consider it their duty to care for older members when the latter are no longer able to care for themselves.

The Ghanaian women recognized that their employers were not kin; yet they redefined the proverb to capture the symbolic and symbiotic nature of their relationships with their employers. Several times during my interviews with the women they referred to "my mother or father that I take care of." By referring to their employers in familial terms, they were giving practical meaning to the proverb. In a sense, the employers were helping the women to "teethe," not in the sense of infantilizing them but in the sense of availing to the women the opportunity to acquire the resources that they needed to achieve their future goals. The women in turn helped the employers to shed their teeth; that is, they gave the employers the comfort and support that they needed in their twilight years. One woman said that she took such good care of her employer that the first few years after his death his children always invited her to their family gatherings. Another woman was disappointed that her employer passed away and his family did not invite her to the funeral. The fact that she was not invited, after taking care of the man for nearly ten years, spoke to the different notions of family and one's responsibility and attachment to it. The woman was baffled when she explained:

> My employer's oldest son was the one who visited him on a regular basis. He would chat with me and make me feel like I was part of the family. And although I did not sit at table with them when they had dinner, I always felt that we were a family and then he passed away and all they were interested in was how much I had to be paid and if they could have my address. I was honestly hurt by their behavior and I have told myself that I will not kill myself to care for anyone like that again. It's not like I'm a robot with no feelings.

The emotional and spiritual investment that the women made in their work speak to the value that they attached to their job. They understood that they were workers, but they also attached an intrinsic quality to their job. After all they cared for human beings; and after several years of living together with their employers they didn't think of their relationships as ones between employers and employees. But that is not how Americans operate. An employee is good to the extent that his or her productive capacity is maximized. An employee is relevant as long as he or she is working. Once the work relationship is broken, there is no relationship. The very name that the women gave to their type of caregiving—private practice—reflected the sense of family that is inherent in the name and the performance of duties. And to the extent that we do not devalue family because of domestic chores, so also did the women not look down upon their work because it is domestic work.

Under-Remuneration: Rose

Scholars and activists have lamented the appallingly low wages that are paid women in domestic care work. The US Department of Labor statistics for 2012 showed that although home care aide came in only second to industrial organizational psychologists on the ten fastest-growing jobs in the economy, it was also the least remunerated on the list. Again in 2014, home care aide appeared among the top ten jobs but there was no change in the income level. Indeed, the annual gross income for home care workers was $20,000.[32] How then could the Ghanaian women claim that 'private practice" paid well? Rose offered an explanation that seemed to undermine the problem of financial exploitation that has been a core concern of experts and scholars. Rose was 35 years, single, with one child in Ghana. She had been a home care worker for twelve years, four of which had been as live-in to a 77-year-old man. During the eight years that she did live-out, she slept in the same room that she sublet from a friend with her then two-year-old daughter. Her schedule changed when she registered with a new agency. Now, instead of working during the day, she worked overnight. That meant she had to find a babysitter for her daughter. That was when she realized that she was simply working to pay someone to care for her daughter. There was very little money left at the end of the month to take care of other needs. And so she decided to send her daughter to Ghana to be cared for by her mother. Rose said she felt guilty sending her daughter to Ghana. She explained: "My daughter was only four years old when I decided to send her home. Several days before she left I couldn't look at her. I felt like I was sending her away because she was being an impediment to my financial well-being. That was a horrible thought that no mother should harbor. It's like thinking that my daughter was a mistake." In her acclaimed edited volume with Barbara Ehrenreich, *Global Woman,* Arlie Russell Hochschild refers to a section of the United Nations Declaration on the Rights of the Child that calls for children to grow under the responsibility of their parents whenever possible.[33] Obviously immigration made taking responsibility for Rose's child's growth impossible. And yet Principle 6 of the same UN provision partly states, "The child, for the full and harmonious development of his [*sic*] personality, needs love and understanding."[34] Here too immigration mediates the UN Declaration. Immigrant care workers must decide whether their own parents (or other family members) in the old country would be better suited to care for children or if nannies should do the care work. It is not by any fluke that many care workers decide to send their children home or leave them behind when they first embark on immigration.

I already noted that in Ghana, being a borger is a big deal; now I must add that being the child of a borger is a bigger deal. A borger's child not only has access to foreign goods, but also lives with the knowledge of being a borger-in-waiting. Importantly, the remittances the parents send are usually the major lifeline for the person taking care of the child. As such caregivers in Ghana take pains to take good care of the "little borgers" and keep them happy so as to continue to receive remittances. And compared to the money that a woman would pay a nanny, a couple of hundred dollars a month can go a long way in Ghana because the US dollar appreciates greatly against the Ghanaian cedi. Immigrant women who leave their children behind or send them home end up performing sacrificial love, an idea that may sound contradictory but that actually reflects the transfer of affection, as theorized by Parrenas and others. In one of her numerous articles on migrant care workers from the Philippines, Parrenas presents the direct views of mothers and children who were separated because the women migrated to engage in care work.[35] One mother recounted how her heart jumped every time the children she cared for called their mother "mama" because that was how her own children called her before she migrated.[36] Care workers denied themselves physical maternal attention and love in order to work so that they and their children would have better futures. The practice is akin to a mother giving up her child for adoption. Most mothers have said that they gave their children up in hopes that the children would get a better home. That was the thinking when Rose decided to send her child to Ghana. It is a tough decision that only the most hard-pressed would make. And that is usually the lot of immigrant women with children.

Once her daughter was gone, Rose decided to work very hard to justify what she thought was a poor but necessary decision. With little education there was not much she could hope to do. She had done live-out and could barely survive on her wages. So she turned to live-in. She maintained her hired room to have a place to keep her things and also sleep on her days off. Asked whether the shift from live-out to live-in was worth the change Rose said, "The employment agency probably made more on me than I made working. I was paid $1200 a month and I had no benefits. I figured that I could make more if I became my own agent and work directly with a client. And guess what, my wages went up to $1800 a month!" She was also given

$20 bonus every two weeks to cover food. Asked how many hours she worked a day Rose indicated that she did not work past 9 p.m. Now, assuming that she started work at 7 a.m. and continued until 9 p. m. she would have worked an average of 14 hours a day. Based on this calculation, Rose made $4.59 an hour, an amount that was lower than the minimum hourly wage in New York in 2010. Rose did regular housework for her client—cook, clean, do laundry. Another woman, Araba, corroborated Rose's account of the start of work for the women. She usually had breakfast ready by 7 a. m. so that her client would have time to attend to her private business. However, unlike Rose, she did not go to bed until 10 p. m. because her client did not go to bed early and Araba had to make sure that the client was safely in bed before she could go to sleep. Her monthly income was $1700. If Araba woke up at 6 a.m., it meant that she worked on average 16 hours a day. That means she was paid roughly $3.80 an hour. When her attention was drawn to that fact, she explained that being in the employer's house did not mean that she was preoccupied with work around the clock. "These are adults we take care of, not children who need constant attention and supervision," she said. Araba explained that unless a client was sick and needed extra care, there was not much to do. It's like living in your own home.

It should also be noted that the women would take home less money in the months that they took some days off. To an outsider not employed in private practice, the wages vis-à-vis hours of work was a clear case of exploitation of the women's labor. Rose did not think so. She explained:

> If you look at live-in this way, you'll think it's a low wage job. But consider this—I don't buy bus tickets for a daily commute; there's no rush hour for me; I don't buy food; I don't even buy toiletries. I get these at my employer's expense. And I do things at my job that I would have done in my own home anyway, only that this time I get paid. Now, what's wrong with that?

Rose made a point that was at the center of intense debate among feminists in the 1970s and 1980s about the value of housework and the need to have it recognized as work and remunerated. Feminist scholars like Maria Rosa Dalla Costa, Wendy Edmond and Suzie Fleming who wrote from a Marxist perspective led the call for housework to be paid work because it supported capitalism.[37] In the summary of her book *Women: A World Survey*, Ruth Sivard stated that if the amount of work women did at home was given economic value, they would add $8 trillion to the global economic output every year.[38] Eight trillion dollars is an impressive amount but Rosemarie Tong points to a weakness in the call for remuneration for housework. If employers were supposed to pay for housework, they would pay both women and their working husbands smaller amounts that in the end would represent a net loss for families.[39] By the 1990s there were counterarguments against the push for remuneration for housework. Some argued that paid housework will not only further isolate women at home; it will also bring government into the home economy and reduce intimate relationships to only their economic value.[40] The two views, the economic potential of housework versus its value in intimate relationships, set up a dichotomy between housewives and all other women. It also separated home care workers from women who did their own housework, thus fracturing the category woman without due recognition to those who got paid for doing housework in all its diversity. There is no doubt that domestic care workers support the capitalist system by relieving middle-class women who would otherwise do housework including nursing the sick and nurturing the young to pursue their careers. There is also no doubt that most domestic care workers have families of their own. What is in doubt is whether or not the advocates for remunerative house chores thought about these women when they pushed their agenda.

Gloria took care of an eighty-year-old widower. She was in her second year taking care of him when I interviewed her. She did live-out with the family until the man lost his wife and then she moved in. Given the man's age and emotional state, Gloria had to be around him most of the time. But then she explained that it was boring because she did nothing most of the time and she was still paid the $2000 she received when she took care of the couple. She revealed that she sent $300 monthly remittance to her children in Ghana, gave her husband $200 toward the family budget and saved $1200 every month. At that rate, she calculated that barring any emergency she could save at least $14,000 a year. Then she asked me: "Can you imagine how much money I will have if I stay employed by the same person for the next five years? Not including what I have now, I will have at least $70,000. Add that to my current savings and I will soon have about $100,000 cash. Tell me that you can save that much as a professor over the same time period!" It did not seem to matter to Gloria or the others whether or not their labor was exploited. In fact, Rose, referred to earlier, did not think that she was exploited at all. Sure, she was on call from early morning until late night, but she did not work every second of the time. She described her chores as light service, by which she meant cooking, doing dishes, cleaning, doing laundry every other day, and vacuuming when necessary. In her estimation, she worked about six hours a day. By that calculation, Rose believed she was paid $10 an hour, which at the time would have been higher than the minimum wage in New York. To some Americans, $100,000 might not seem like a lot of money; however, the women did not think of their earning power in the American context. The exchange value of the US dollar against the Ghanaian cedi was about 3:1 ratio at the time I interviewed the women. With proper planning and depending on location in Ghana a person who had $100,000 liquid cash in

2010 could build a decent house and still have money left to start a trade if they so desired.

The women mentioned above were naturalized and looked at their job in the long term. Four others, among them Mrs. Osei, were temporary legal residents on visitors' visas. They were part of a group of women who would secure visitors' visas and once in the US find temporary work. They would return to Ghana to shore up their businesses or start something new. Home care became popular among these women. Some did childcare for Ghanaian families and those who were lucky, like Mrs. Osei, got to do live-in. These women were usually waged workers in Ghana who accumulated leave days and then came to the US to work for short periods. Mrs. Osei was excited to relieve a live-in worker for two months; after that stint she secured her own client. Like Lydia, she had to decide whether to go back to Ghana and continue with her work or overstay her visa and accumulate dollars. In her case the decision was easy; she was going to be paid $1800 a month as a caregiver which, when exchanged into cedis, could be more than her combined gross salary for three months. She decided to take the job and write home to her employer to extend her leave without pay. Mrs. Osei said of her job: "For six months straight I worked without any time off. Some of the people I knew thought I already left for Ghana. But I was right here in the US. I came home when my client went on a two week vacation and she would not allow me to stay in her house." Mrs. Osei's hope was that she would be able to work for at least three years to be able to save about $50,000. That would be enough money to start a trading business in Ghana in case she did not get her job back. Like the other women, she calculated that she could save $1500 a month.

Stories such are these became a powerful magnet that attracted women to live-in caregiving, whether they were already in the US or in Ghana. Recalling the economic conditions that motivated her immigration in the first place, Rose said that her family was poor and being the only one to travel abroad, the pressure was on her to change the family's circumstance. Her intention was to build a modern house for her mother and siblings, start a poultry farm for her younger brother and then get a store for herself. These investments would require substantial sums of money. Rose then invoked an old Akan adage that literally translates, "if you know the source of your fountain, you go with your calabash in hand." Rose understood the enormity of her responsibility toward her family by virtue of being an immigrant. She would have to work hard and without interruption. Live-in offered her that opportunity. In light of what she was up against, questions about exploitation took second place in her reckoning.

Isolation: Aminata

Loneliness doesn't happen to only live-in care workers. Many new immigrants, especially if they traveled alone, go through an initial period of loneliness, even when they live with others. When there is no one to talk to although there are people around you, or when no one seems interested in what you are doing, and you are in a place so far away from home, you lose your sense of self. I know this because I experienced it. Therefore when scholars emphasize isolation as a serious problem that live-in care workers experience, they address an issue that has emotional and psychological impact on women. Somehow, for some immigrant women, isolation may be a welcome relief. We remember Aminata as the abused wife who, unlike the other women, went into homecare work shortly after her arrival in the US. Her client was a married man, 75 years old, quite robust, and demanding. Although she was supposed to work for only the man, she ended up working for two. The house was big and the couple wanted it cleaned every day. Other than grocery shopping, Aminata did all the work in the house. Asked if she was not overwhelmed with work, Aminata quipped,

> What work? Cleaning the bath tub or vacuuming the floor? Remember I told you that I was a trader in Ghana? If you sat in one of those vehicles loaded with goods and made the overnight trip from my town to Accra, you won't call what I do here work. When I do laundry, I toss the items into the machine. When I have piled up plates and bowls, I put them in the dishwasher. And the people I take care of like to go out a lot so most afternoons I'm home alone.

She had her living quarters in the fully furnished basement where she could cook her own meals when she was tired of eating what she called "white people's food." She was paid $1800 monthly but she was going to ask for an increase since she was working for two. Had she planned to make this request until she was asked about the hours she worked in a day? It was not even clear if Aminata understood the relationship between her wages and the hours she put in daily. She was relieved that she had a safe place where she was not yelled at, pushed around, or punched. Her basement apartment was her sanctuary, where she would be alone and safe. Unlike Elsie who thought being put in the basement was an affront to her dignity, Aminata found the isolation in the basement most welcoming. She would not have to communicate with her employers if she did not have to, and she could connect with her friends via phone without any interruption once she retired to her basement sanctuary. Importantly, she controlled her earnings. She could send money to her parents anytime she wanted without having to explain to her husband why doing so was necessary. She stopped paying for her sponsorship five months into her job as a live-in care worker. Aminata compared her before and after immigration life and concluded that at least for the time being, live-in was her best option. She intended to continue taking good care of her clients so that she would be there for a very long time. She was not divorced, not even officially separated, but her work created a physical and symbolic separation between herself and her husband to a degree that suggested she was single.

If Aminata welcomed her isolation, it was because of her marital situation. The others neither complained of nor welcomed isolation because there was no need to. There was also no cultural explanation for their apparent lack of sense of isolation. It should be noted, first, that the women generally created a congenial work environment. Most had done live-out care work and knew how lonely it could become if the relationship between employer and employee stayed strictly business-like. And while there were individual variations in how they related to their employers, by and large the women felt connected due to the nature of their work. In most cases, there were only two people at home. Surely, there would be interaction even if for brief moments. The women also had families, friends, and a larger immigrant community that they could connect with. And thanks to technology, the women did not have to have physical contact with the world outside their work sites to feel connected.

The women's stories speak to sacrifice, resilience, endurance, and selfless devotion that characterize and generally shape women's experiences regardless of the economic activity they engage in. The Ghanaian women might have been aware of subtle forms of exploitation and abuse at their work place, and they might have understood that mainstream American society did not accord live-in care work much respect, but ultimately, it was their perception and not how others perceived care work that mattered. Importantly, the women considered the economic benefit of their work in relation to any vulnerabilities they might have faced and determined that the money they made compensated for any adverse experiences associated with the work.

NOTES

1. Human Rights Watch, "Hidden in the Home," 30.
2. Human Rights Watch, "Maid to Order: Ending Abuses against Migrant Domestic Workers in Singapore, Dec 6, 2005, https://www.hrw.org/report/2005/12/06/maid-order/ending-abuses-against-migrant-domestic-workers-singapore; Pierrette Hondagneu-Sotelo, "Blowups and Other Unhappy Endings," in *Global Woman: Nannies, Maid, and Sex Workers in the New Economy,* edited by Barbara Ehrenreich and Arlie R. Hochschild (New York: Metropolitan Books, 2002), 55–69; Lynn May-Rivas, "Invisible Labors: Caring for the Independent Person," in *Global Woman: Nannies, Maid, and Sex Workers in the New Economy,* eds., Barbara Ehrenreich and Arlie R. Hochschild (New York: Metropolitan Books, 2002), 70–84.
3. Al-Seyassah, "Torture disables Maid, Kuwait couple acquitted," *Kuwait Times,* March 19, 2017, http://www.timeskuwait.com/Times_Torture-disables-maid-Kuwaiti-couple-acquittedhttp://www.timeskuwait.com/Times_Torture-disables-maid-Kuwaiti-couple-acquitted.

4. "Filipina maid dies in botched escape," *Kuwait Times*, March 21, 2017, http://news.kuwaittimes.net/filipina-maid-dies-in-botched-escape/.

5. Yahoo Newsroom, "Another Maid falls to her Death in Serangoon," May 18, 2012, https://sg.news.yahoo.com/another-maid-falls-to-her-death-in-serangoon.html.

6. Human Rights Watch, "Hidden in the Home: Abuse of Domestic Workers with Special Visas in the United States," 13, no. 2 (G) (June 2001): 1–54.

7. Barbara Ehrenreich and Arlie R. Hochschild, eds. *Global Woman: Nannies, Maids and Sex Workers in the New Economy* (New York: Holt Paperbacks, 2002).

8. Human Rights Watch, "Hidden in the Home," 7; United States Court of Appeal, First Circuit: United States of America, *Appellee v. Talal H. Alzanki*, Defendant, Appellant, No. 94–1645.

9. Human Rights Watch, "Hidden in the Home," 9.

10. Human Rights Watch, "Singapore: Domestic Workers Suffer Grave Abuses," December 7, 2005, https://www.hrw.org/news/2005/12/07/singapore-domestic-workers-suffer-grave-abuses.

11. Stefani Bonato and McKenna Coll, "Domestic Workers' Rights in the United States," A report prepared for the U.N. Human Rights Committee in response to the Second and Third Periodic Report of the United States, n.d., 3; Human Rights Watch, "Hidden in the Home," 16.

12. Alyssa Newcomb, "Washington Couple could face Decades in Prison for Adopted Daughter's Death," ABC News, September 10, 2013, http://abcnews.go.com/US/washington-couple-face-decades-prison-death-adopted-daughter/story?id=20216426.

13. Byrd, "The Dirty Side of Domestic Work," 247; Human Rights watch, "Hidden in the Home," 20–21.

14. Domestic workers on contract are expected find work within the expiration of their contract or to have a grace period of 30 days within which to find another position or to leave the country immediately. Domestic workers working on contract to international bodies like the IMF expect worker to leave the US immediately if they break the contract. For more details see Human Rights Watch, "Hidden in the Home," 26.

15. Private Practice: Show Summary," http://www.tv.com/shows/private-practice/.

16. Lynn May-Rivas, "Invisible Labors: Caring for the Independent Person," in *Global Woman: Nannies, Maid, and Sex Workers in the New Economy,* eds., Barbara Ehrenreich and Arlie R. Hochschild (New York: Metropolitan Books, 2002), 76.

17. Premilla Nadasen, "Citizenship Rights, Domestic Work, and the Fair Labor Standards Act," *The Journal of Policy History* 24, no. 2 (2012): 74–94.

18. See Dolen Perkins-Valdez's historical novel *Wench* (New York: HarperCollins, 2010) for parallels between Nancy's narrative and the riveting story of slave women who had amorous relationships with their masters. I am by no means suggesting that the Ghanaian women's work and/or relationships with their employers approximated slavery; I am suggesting that the promise of wealth can lead a worker to ignore the conditions surrounding the work.

19. I worked in a plastics manufacturing company in Toronto where the separation Elsie described was a taken-for-granted issue. The front of the huge glass building

housed the offices that were occupied by white staff. Offices were well decorated and ventilated; they were also very clean. A little side door opened to the huge factory floor with large machines spewing out fumes from melting plastic. Workers were mostly from Ghana, India, and Jamaica. The windows did not open and the heat from the machines was so high that giant air conditioning units were placed at strategic points to keep workers cool. I was paid $7 an hour. I was fired from this job when I sought permission from my line supervisor to attend an academic conference. He said I was researching the company under false pretense and I was fired.

20. Pierrette Hondagneu-Sotelo, "Blowups and Other Unhappy Endings," in *Global Woman: Nannies, Maid, and Sex Workers in the New Economy*, eds., Barbara Ehrenreich and Arlie R. Hochschild (New York: Metropolitan Books, 2002), 55–69.

21. Akua prepared food for several days, cleaned the house, did the laundry, and then in the evening told him that she would be gone for four days. Another person would take care of him in her absence. She said her employer was happy to see her back after four days, although she thought that he was going to ask her to leave.

22. Lois A. Bowers, "Assisted Living Resident Allegedly Raped," *Springfield News-Leader*, April 2, 2017, http://www.bing.com/search?q=seniors+in+assisted+living+facilities+raped&src=IE-SearchBox&FORM=IESR02.

23. Chris Serres, "Senior's Rape Throws Light on Problems in Assisted Living Homes," *Star Tribune*, March 27, 2014, http://www.startribune.com/senior-s-rape-throws-light-on-problems-in-assisted-living-homes/252567371/.

24. Bowers, "Assisted Living Resident Raped."

25. Valerie Van Booven, "Joplin, Missouri Home Care Aide Accused of Stealing from Client's Debit Card," HomeCareDaily.com, December 6, 2016, https://www.homecaredaily.com/2015/12/06/missouri-home-care-aide-accused-of-stealing-from-clients-debit-card/.

26. WDRB.com, "In-home Caregiver Accused of Stealing Jewelry from Louisville Client," March 20, 2014, http://www.wdrb.com/story/25027370/in-home-caregiver-accused-of-stealing-jewelry-from-louisville-client.

27. Steve Mosco, "Aide Steals $800,000 from Elderly Patient," *Times Ledger*, May 9, 2012, http://www.timesledger.com/stories/2012/19/homehealthaide_fh_2012_05_10_q.html.

28. Mosco, "Aide Steals $800,000."

29. Hondagneu-Sotelo, "Blowups," 61.

30. Clare Ungerson, *Policy is Personal: Sex, Gender and Informal Care* (London: Tavistock, 1987).

31. Sankofa, Ghanaian Chicago Community, "How Many Excuses, Asiedu Nketia? NPP-USA Women's Wing," http://sankofaonline.com/archives/31101.

32. US Department of Labor, Labor Statistics, 2012 and 2014, https://www.dol.gov/.

33. Arlie Russell Hochschild, "Love and Gold," in *Global Woman: Nannies, Maids, Sex Workers and the New Economy*, eds., Barbara Ehrenreich and Arlie Russell Hochschild. (New York: Metropolitan Books, 2002), 15; UNICEF, "Declaration of the Rights of the Child, 1959," https://www.unicef.org/malaysia/1959-Declaration-of-the-Rights-of-the-Child.pdf.

34. UNICEF, "Declaration of the Rights of the Child, 1959."

35. Rhacel Salazar Parrenas, "The Care Crisis in the Philippines: Children and Transnational Families in the New Global Economy," in *Global Woman: Nannies, Maids, Sex Workers and the New Economy,* eds., Barbara Ehrenreich and Arlie Russell Hochschild. (New York: Metropolitan Books, 2002), 39–54.

36. Parrenas, "The Care Crisis in the Philippines," 41.

37. Wendy Edmond and Suzie Fleming, "If Women were Paid for all They Do," in *All Work and No Pay: Women, Housework, and the Wages Due*, ed. Wendy Edmond and Suzie Fleming (London: Power of Women Collective and Falling Wall Press, 1975), 5–12; Maria Rosa Dalla Costa, "A General Strike," in *All Work and No Pay: Women, Housework, and the Wages Due*, ed. Wendy Edmond and Suzie Fleming (London: Power of Women Collective and Falling Wall Press, 1975), 125–127; Heidi Hartmann, "The Unhappy Marriage of Marxism and Feminism: Toward a More Progressive Union," in *Feminist Theory Reader: Local and Global Perspectives,* Carole R. McCann and Seung-Kyung Kim, eds. (New York: Routledge, 2013), 189.

38. Ruth Leger Sivard, *Women: A World Survey* (Washington, DC: World Priorities, 1995), 5.

39. Rosemary Tong, *Feminist Thought*, 4th ed. (Boulder, CO.: Westview Press, 2014), 106–7.

40. Victoria Robinson and Diane Richardson, *Introducing* Women's *and Gender Studies*, 4ed (London: Palgrave, 2010), 208.

Chapter 6

Organizing Family from a Distance

One of the key issues that working women with families face is dealing with the work-family conflict. The conflict describes how family responsibilities intrude upon work in the public sphere and vice versa. When women work in the public realm and then come home to assume responsibility for domestic chores, they are said to be doing a double day or second shift. The double day places enormous stress on women. Whether they work part- or full-time, women with families go home to cook, clean, launder, make beds, bathe children, read/sing to them before bed, do the dishes, etc. By the time they go to bed, women are completely exhausted. They wake up the next morning and repeat the same routine without fail. The double day thus creates tension not only between a woman and her remunerative labor but also between her and other members of the household as she demands their participation in house chores to ease her exhaustion.

Women have adopted several strategies to deal with the problem. Some take part-time jobs in order to release time to care for their families. Others give up their jobs temporarily to deal with family issues and then rejoin the workforce once the situation eases or is solved. Some make personal sacrifices in terms of what is important for the institutions they work for versus what is important in safeguarding their own positions on the job. They sacrifice personal advantages that are key to promotion in modern careers in order to be with their families. Some women give up work altogether and devote their time to working at home while others hire other women to care for their families as they devote their full attention to their careers. Within this complex web of the work-family dynamic are immigrant live-in care workers. They are at the center of care work, but they can only care for their own families from the margins. This is because unlike other female workers who go home at the end of their workdays to be with their families, live-in caregivers do not have that privilege. Thus, although they are faced with the same family challenges that other married women in the work force face, they must, of necessity, adopt different strategies to deal with the family-work tension. Their job and class positions preclude them from adopting the strategies identified above. Because live-in caregivers do not go home at the end of the work day, an analysis of the management of their families that is couched within the framework of the double day cannot explain the dynamics of such management. This is because of the transnational character of the immigrant family. Thus I suggest triple management as a conceptual and analytical framework that can adequately explain the multi-layered family structures that live-in care workers must relate to from the remoteness of their work places. These family structures include the immediate family, the immigrant community, and the family left in the home country.

In her study of Filipino domestic workers in Los Angeles and Rome, Rhacel Salazar Parrenas describes the transnational family in terms of dislocation. She notes that dislocation occurred when the women were separated from family members in the Philippines and marginalized in the Filipino diasporic communities. The result was that the women felt alienated.[1] Building on Parrenas's characterization of the transnational family, triple management recognizes the separation of families and the presence of an immigrant community, but it does so from a perspective of embeddedness instead of alienation or dislocation, and places the women squarely within the family structures regardless of the women's physical location. Triple management also goes beyond domestic chores that undergird the second shift and emphasizes relationships and the best ways to cultivate them. Inherent in the conceptualization of triple management is the de-emphasis of gender roles as the motive force of tension and a focus on interpersonal relationships with spouses, children, community members, and families in Ghana. As we will see shortly, the women had to carefully devise strategies to meet the needs of all the family constituents, and some of the strategies did not involve the performance of domestic chores at all.

Family plays a crucial role in the lives of immigrant women. It eases the problem of isolation, especially in the first weeks of arrival in a new country. It facilities networking and also gives immigrants a sense of belonging. To immigrant women, family goes beyond the nuclear units that we are accustomed to as Americans. Family undergoes changes due to the process of migration and women have to relate to them in different ways to make their lives meaningful, especially in a country where skin color interacts with gender to limit immigrant women's lives. People who had lived in nuclear family units in their home countries may find themselves living with other family members in what sociologist Judith Stacey calls the accordion family.[2] According to Stacey, the accordion family describes the expansion and contraction of the size of the family unit as extended members enter and leave depending on their needs and the capabilities of the family.[3] Conversely, people who lived in extended family systems may find themselves in nuclear units when they migrate, separated from other members in the old country. This process of separation creates the transnational family.

Immigration also forges hybridized families among people who are related neither by blood nor by marriage. This type of "family" is formed based purely on friendships and includes people from different racial or ethnic backgrounds. Whites are noted for forming hybridized families with immigrants when they 'adopt' the immigrants into their families. The adult members become nanas and grandpas, aunties, and uncles to children while the children see each other as cousins. There is also what one can identify as the diasporic family that forms within the same ethnic community. Individuals who share the same "cultural" motifs or identifiers such as membership in a church, alumni of particular academic institutions, or people from the same town form associations that function as family to members as well as their respective constituents in Ghana.[4] These cultural associations, as they are called, can be found in major cities in countries where Ghanaian immigrants reside.[5] Some of these associations organize across national borders, like the Council of Brong Ahafo Associations in North America. Superimposed on all these diasporic family forms is the larger immigrant community. Immigration somehow changes national identity into an ethnic category, as in the phrase "Ghanaian immigrants." Ghana becomes an ethnic identifier for immigrants who come from that country, although Ghana is multi-ethnic and multicultural and Ghanaians generally prefer to identify themselves first by their ethnic background before the national identity. The erasure of the diversity of immigrants' cultural background at the level of the state (the immigrant-receiving country) creates yet another layer of community that immigrants must identify with.

Then there is family left behind in Ghana. There is the expectation among family members, regardless of ethnicity, that those who are fortunate to become persons of means ought to help less fortunate members. Since immigrants are perceived to have access to resources that non-immigrant family members do not have access to, the immigrants are assumed to be rich and therefore expected to do something in or for the family. That could mean repairing an old house or building a new one altogether; it could also mean taking up the financial responsibility of a member in school or sending money to cover the expense of an illness or funeral.[6] In most cases, when women travel as independent migrants, those with children leave the children behind until they are fully established in the new country before they are reunited with the children. Others send their children to Ghana when combining work and nurturing becomes too much to handle. Once women send their children to Ghana, their responsibility to family moves beyond benevolence to that of long-distance mothers who must devise ways to stay connected with their children and the family members taking care of the children.

To the Ghanaian immigrant woman, family is not a single entity that she must relate to. Family is multi-layered and functions at different sites. As such family relationships go well beyond the performance of chores to expectations and obligations that can be appreciated from the perspective of the immigrant. How the Ghanaian women upheld the relationships is the focus of the sections that follow.

ORGANIZING IMMEDIATE FAMILY

For married care workers, the most difficult part of their work was management of their immediate families from their remote work sites. They were well aware that immigration had changed a lot of things about the family but not gender roles. They were responsible for house chores before they took up jobs as live-in care workers and they did not expect that their jobs would somehow alter their roles in the family. They would continue to perform domestic chores as expected of them when they visited home on their days off. Their real concern was maintaining relationships with their husbands and children. The men understood that their wives were doing live-in for the good of their families; however, some were not prepared for the long periods that the women stayed on the job before they took days off. These were difficult positions to reconcile. Women were not paid when they took days off; so the question became how long they could stay on before they went on break and how many days they could afford to stay away from work.

Maame Esi had been separated from her husband, Kwadwo, for twelve years before she joined him with their two teenaged sons. She had the equivalent of a high school diploma and worked in an office for several years in Ghana. She expected to find an office job when she arrived in the US, but with her educational background, it was difficult for her to do so. She had plans to go to school to become a registered nurse but since she had been out of school for so long, she rather underwent a three-month course to obtain her Certified Nursing Assistant (CNA) certification. Once certified, she had a job in a nursing home on an overnight schedule. She worked from 11 p.m. to 7 a. m and got home when the boys and her husband had already left for school and work respectively. She also worked six days a week. Asked why she took such a schedule, Maame Esi explained, "It was always very quiet when I came home so I had enough time to sleep. I would wake up around 1 p.m. and cook if necessary. We would have dinner around 6 p.m. then I'll catch some quick sleep from 7:30 to 10 and get ready to go back to work. That schedule worked very well for me." Clearly work stood in the way of family togetherness. Maame Esi was home but her presence was not felt by other family members. In fact, Sunday was the only day in the week that the entire family were together.

Nevertheless, Maame Esi changed her job and took a live-in position because she claimed working in a nursing home was tough work. She could not handle dealing with bodily emissions and lifting heavy bodies. Her desire to be a nurse also fizzled out. It was all about work and the money she could make, and private practice appeared to be far more "decent" than work in a nursing home. Maame Esi sacrificed the intimacy and synergy that held families together for work that detached her from her family. But why would she adopt such an attitude? Like most of the women in the study, she used her life in Ghana as the yardstick against which to measure her progress in the US. She considered herself middle class in Ghana, by virtue of being an office worker and did not want to return to Ghana below her perceived status. The irony was that Maame Esi underwent a class shift from her middle-class position in Ghana to a nondescript position defined by her immigrantness. Parrenas referred to this "contradictory class mobility" as one of the dislocations that Filipino domestic care workers experienced in Italy and the US.[7] In Maame Esi's case, the loss in status in the US would be restored in the long term if she went back to Ghana with some kind of outlook. The urge to prove herself invariably affected the organization of her family. It was that "thinking back" attitude that partly defined her familial relationships.

There were other things Maame Esi did that weakened her ties to her family. She arranged with her employer to visit her family every six weeks. She knew that her husband could not visit her at her workplace, and staying away for long periods of time could further strain her relationship with him and the boys. Her view was that she waited twelve years before she was united with her husband; for him, to wait for forty days at a time would not kill him. They needed money to undertake some projects in Ghana and that called for sacrifices. She did not mention her children's education or the possibility of buying a house in the US. As she talked about sacrifices, Maame Esi made sure that she stayed in close contact with her family through phone calls. She called mostly at night when she had finished her work and her client had retired to his room. She said that her conversations with her sons were deep at first. They reminisced about life in Ghana, they compared aspects of Ghanaian and American cultures, etc. Gradually, the conversations changed. The boys became detached and would respond to her questions in monosyllables, always having an excuse to end a conversation. She concluded that they were growing and had other interests other than talking to their mother every night. Maame Esi's penchant to rationalize her behavior became a strong strategic option that she used time and again as she organized her family from a distance.

Her conversations with her husband were sometimes heated. He did not like being called late at night because it disturbed his sleep; if she did not call at all he complained of being neglected. She did not want him to call during her work hours because it might make her employer angry; if he did not pick her calls right away it was a sign that he was talking to another woman. These conflicting signals showed the extent to which work-mediated family life without the tension caused by the performance of house chores. The couple, but Maame Esi in particular, did not want family to interfere with their work. That attitude again reflected a transnational ordering or regressive pattern of thinking that linked their lives and work in the US to expectations in Ghana.[8] These women straddled two worlds where one was an extraction point and the other was the point of deposit. To maximize their output in one world and input in the other required a struggle whose turf was the immediate family. And given the central role that women play in families, the Ghanaian women were caught in a situation that required careful balancing and strategizing. One action that seemed to work for Maame Esi was psychological preparation of her family members for her days off. She recalled that she made such a big deal of her first visit home after taking up her job that there was great anticipation on both sides. She said: "Going home felt like a reunion. The boys [that included her husband] had prepared for my arrival. They had cleaned the house and cooked dinner. They all seemed very happy to see me and I was overwhelmed. In fact, I thought to myself if staying away from the family for such long periods was the right thing to do."

In spite of her mental struggle, Maame Esi did not quit her job. Instead, she used her days off to reposition herself as the center of the family, drawing everybody into the circle through endless conversation, cooking, cleaning, and making sure that everybody was well fed. Saturdays were her busy days on her days off work. She would prepare a quick lunch and then start cooking for what she called the long term. She said: "I cannot expect one meal to last for six weeks for three healthy men with good appetites. I usually prepare different dishes—soups, stews and rice—over two days. These are the ones meant for the freezer. I also cook other meals just for the weekend and a dish that I would take with me to work." Maame Esi would dish the food in meal sizes and arrange them neatly in the freezer. That way, all the men had to do in her absence was decide what to eat and food was ready. They did not have to eat the same meal at the same time; each person decided what they wanted.

Kwadwo, Maame Esi's husband and one of the three men who participated in the study, held a slightly different version of his wife's visits. He admitted that she cooked and cleaned but then said that it was her duty to perform those chores. He claimed that his wife came home only when there was an event happening on Saturday night that they had to attend. As far as he was concerned, his wife did not take days off work because she wanted to be with her own family; she took time off to interact in the community. He also complained that when they went out Saturday nights, Maame Esi would stay until dawn only to come home and sleep for about three hours and then get ready for church. That meant much of Saturday night was spent out and part of Sunday was spent in church. In his estimation, the family did not have much quality time with her during her days of visit.

Another woman, Yaa, had similar problems with her husband. Her daughter was five years old when she took up her live-in job. Her husband did not know how to cook but she thought he would learn; he also did not appear to be bothered taking care of a five-year-old girl in her absence. What appeared to cause tension was figuring out a way to meet their sexual needs. Yaa had worked out an eight-week schedule of work followed by a week's break when her client would be with his family. She said she sensed trouble when, just three weeks after moving to her work site, her husband sent their daughter to a friend and then drove over to her place of work for a visit. Apparently he did not know that she could not receive visitors let alone have one stay for an entire weekend. Yaa could not even receive him in the house; they sat outside to have a conversation. It was bad enough that as a man he did the housework as well as take care of a young girl. Now, if he would be denied his sexual needs, then where was the marriage? He did not understand how a prisoner could have conjugal rights with his wife in prison and he could not even get the privilege of sitting in a couch in a living room when he visited his wife. Yaa felt guilty when her husband raised these poignant issues. Then she revealed why she negotiated her schedule the way she did: "My husband was that type of man who refused to be responsible for any kind of housework. He did not understand how a woman who did not do the laundry by hand, walk to fetch water or firewood or even pound fufu, should ask her husband to help around the house. What the @#$% did she expect a man to?" That did it for Yaa. She could have changed her schedule but decided against it.

Yaa's decision to work for two months before visiting her own family suggested that she was either protesting or punishing her husband for his refusal to do housework, although taking care of a five-year-old was housework, a fact that Yaa completely ignored. But that was only a small part of a complicated issue. Yaa's behavior points to two ways in which immigration can mediate cultural norms and empower women. Until fairly recently, most Ghanaian men did not do housework, unless they were servants or lived alone. Education and travel are slowly causing changes in men's view of housework, but generally, men do not perform domestic chores. Not surprisingly, Ghanaian women have owned domestic work. They may perform it themselves, do it with their children, or hire girls or other women to do their housework. What happens then when Ghanaians migrate to another culture where men's performance of domestic work is encouraged and embraced?

Immigration can engender changes in the family in regard to domestic work and the change must happen to both women and men. Men should accept their performance of house chores as integral to the health of the family and women must relax their hold over the domestic sphere as their special preserve. Undergirding this synergistic approach to the performance of domestic chores is the bigger question of decision making in the family. Who should ask men to step up to certain domestic responsibilities? On what would that power rest to instruct men? These questions point to women as the agents of change in the family, a proposition that calls attention to renowned sociologist Anthony Gidden's theory of structuration.[9] In a comment on the theory, David Gauntlett explains:

> human agency and social structure are in a relationship with each other, and it is the repetition of the acts of individual agents which reproduces the structure. This means that there is a social structure—traditions, institutions, moral codes, and established ways of doing things; but it also means that these can be changed when people start to ignore them, replace them, or reproduce them differently.[10]

Using this theory as a guide, we see that the Ghanaian women reproduced but also altered their roles as wives against the backdrop of their jobs as live-in caregivers. In the process, men were forced to adapt to the changing family dynamics. The women did not refuse to perform their assigned roles; they just were not home to perform them. When they took time off work husbands and wives reverted to their expected gender roles, as exemplified by Maame Esi's narrative above. Yaa's husband, on the other hand, appeared to be making a plea that had little to do with house work. He seemed to feel neglected and isolated but Yaa pretended not to understand. She said she would go home to find the laundry basket piled up, fridge empty, bathroom all messed up, and her husband's explanation was that he was waiting for her to come home so they would clean together. Initially, Yaa found it romantic that her husband wanted them to clean together. But it soon dawned on her that it was not because he wanted to clean with her; it was a way to keep her home when she came for visits. When there was cleaning to do, she would not have time to visit with friends. If she understood his silent plea, she ignored it. Yaa's husband decided to take a vacation about three years after she took her live-in job. He went to Ghana with the young girl who was then eight years, intending to spend only six weeks. At the time of my interview with Yaa, her husband had been in Ghana with the girl for eight years. She had visited them three times during the eight years. Yaa had appealed to her husband to return, if it meant quitting her job.

When we factor children into women's organization of family, a different scenario emerges. Aminata, for example, did not have children to worry about and she was married to a man who she appeared to fear. She did not call him or go home often. Maame Esi, on the other hand, had two teenaged sons and tried to stay in touch with them through nightly phone calls; however, as the boys settled into American life, their interactions with her diminished and became detached. Maame Esi rationalized her weak relationship with her children by appealing to their sense of growth. Women who had young children had to decide between paying for others to care for the children or sending the children home to be cared for by other family members, usually their mothers. The practice of sending children home was not restricted to women in live-in domestic arrangements. It is widespread in the Ghanaian immigrant community and reflects the common practice of kin fostering in Ghana.[11]

The married women's confidence in dealing with their husbands on a seemingly equal footing rested on one thing: they were contributing handsomely to the family economy. Indeed, some of the women had joint savings with their husbands so that they would jointly undertake projects in Ghana and take care of children. Women's financial capital positioned them to be equal power brokers in their families but as we will see later, being positioned to act a certain way did not always translate into concrete action. Women's long absences from home potentially gave their spouses access to the family budget without women's knowledge or consent.

Maintaining Community Presence

Among Ghanaians, belonging is very important. One must belong to a group or groups in order to tap into the group's resources. That contrasts with the individualism that characterizes American life. Transitions in life that might be considered private in American social life, such as a birth or death, are celebrated by an entire community of people in Ghana. Death epitomizes this kind of transition. It is the height of human suffering in more than one aspect. It brings loss, debt, and grief. Unless it is the death of a child, an entire community will come together for a funeral where there is collective grieving and also cash donations to the bereaved family to defray debts they might have incurred. Immigrants have carried over some of the traditions and modified them. For example, funerals that are held during daytime in Ghana are held at night to suit circumstances in the US. It is understood that death will occur to community members or to family members in Ghana. Should one bear the burden of grief alone in private or seek collective grief to lessen the burden? Would one be able to singularly bear the financial burden of death in a foreign country? If a person did not have any family and she died, who would be responsible for the body? These are important questions that guide community dynamics and people's interactions with each other.

The good thing is that there are associations and organizations and "families" that can support women only if they participate in them. These organizations offer programs that support members and often non-members as well. The churches are the quintessential community organizations that offer spiritual as well as social support to members and the larger Ghanaian immigrant community. Some churches have fully furnished gyms where church members work out for free; others have halls that they rent out to the public for social events at reduced cost. Churches have vans and buses that shuttle members without means of transportation to their events. They also give out amounts of money to members when they lose a child, spouse, or parent regardless of the residence of the deceased. Churches organize crusades, musical shows and all night prayer sessions in addition to regular Sunday services. Most Ghanaian immigrants join churches for the support and socialization. In addition to the churches, there are cultural associations and private clubs that organize events for members as well as support individual members in times of need. Community events are organized on Saturdays to enable the greater number of people to patronize.

One of the major community events is the funeral. It has become a tradition among Ghanaian immigrants to organize funerals for parents who died in Ghana. For some, organizing a funeral is a way to recoup money they had donated to others over the course of time. Others organize funerals to defray the huge costs they incurred when they went to Ghana to bury a dead parent. Also of note, and perhaps most important to many Ghanaian immigrants, is the fact that it is considered a disgrace to bury a deceased adult abroad. The problem is that shipping a dead body to Ghana is very expensive. Unless a family is wealthy or the deceased person left money to cover shipment, community assistance is the only way that some will be able to send dead relatives home. For these reasons people join associations—churches, town, ethnic associations and special clubs as a form of social security.

The organization of a social event in the community has its unique dynamics that only Ghanaian immigrants will appreciate. Regardless of the event—funeral, birthday, or wedding—crowd size is of utmost importance. The larger the crowd, the better. It shows solidarity, popularity, and the possibility of financial gain. Indeed, some Ghanaians believe that a person's worth in life is reflected by the size of the crowd at that person's funeral. The beliefs and expectations surrounding social events mean that an immigrant must be active in the community. An active community member is a visible community member. This is where live-in caregiving can potentially adversely affect women. Women might make donations through spouses or friends and pay association dues; however, these fine gestures would be known only to the recipients of the money. The larger community would not necessarily know about these efforts.

Live-in caregivers knew all these dynamics in the community. They tried to avoid invisibility and potential loss of community resources by arranging their days off work to coincide with events that were close to them. They would attend church if they were Christians, visit friends, shop at Ghanaian grocery stores, and by doing so, they achieved a measure of exposure than might be considered acceptable in the community. In addition to the churches, women actively participated in the programs of the hometown associations by paying their monthly dues, attending fundraisers to support a cause in Ghana and attending the annual picnics for fun and "family" get-together. Fortunately for the women, these community events are organized on Saturdays so they would arrange their days off to include weekends in order for them to fully participate in the events. One of the women described her conundrum when she decided to perform her father's funeral. She was married with children, she also had a hybridized family but she was not very well known in the community at large. Instead of using her own name to announce the funeral, she used her husband's. The flyer, featuring a bold picture of her husband in mourning cloth, read: "Mr. Asamoah cordially invites you to the home going celebration of his dear father-in-law..." Mr. Asamoah was very well known because of his membership in multiple associations. He would be able to draw a crowd if he was listed as the chief mourner. To an outsider without knowledge of the internal dynamics of the Ghanaian immigrant community, the woman's action would typify her subordinate position to her husband. That view may be accurate in a broader patriarchal context, but in this case, the conscious transfer of the woman's position as the chief mourner to her husband was caused by her work as live-in caregiver. One can only imagine what would have happened if the woman was not married or did not belong to a diasporic family.

Connecting with Family in Ghana

The proliferation of new technology, particularly in the past two decades, has created some kind of amnesia regarding how people kept in touch with each other. Cell phones and social media that are common forms of communication today were not in widespread use in the closing years of the twentieth century even in a highly technological country like the US. Technology that was reserved for the rich and those in big business is now widely available and at affordable prices too. I can now sit in my living room and do face time with my mother in a rural town in Ghana. Twenty years ago that was unthinkable. If I wanted to talk to my mother, I would call to the post office and leave a message to be forwarded to her. There was no guarantee that the message would be delivered. I relied on the goodwill of the clerk. There was also no way to tell if the clerk met my mother when he went to deliver the message. And so I would make a follow-up call the next day. Sometimes I was lucky; she would be waiting. Other times I would be told that she was not home when the message was delivered. I could arrange phone calls because there was a post office in my town where everybody knew everybody else. Unless they had private lines, people who came from large towns or cities and those from areas where there were no postal services could not use post offices to talk to family members. By the early 2000s communication centers had sprung up, and calling Ghana was no longer difficult, except in very remote areas where there was no electricity. Because of these initial limitations, transnational mothers' first strategy of staying in touch with their children and other family members was through letters. Occasionally, though, letters would go missing in Ghana, especially when some unscrupulous postal staff suspected they might contain foreign currency. Letters also took some time to be delivered. But most of all, there had to be someone around to read once a letter was delivered, unless the other mother was literate. In villages and small towns, that meant calling in the postmaster, catechist, or teacher.

By the beginning of the twenty-first century, technology had revolutionized communication in Ghana. Communication centers sprung up in all corners and made it possible for people abroad to stay in touch with family. Rose, for instance, said that she loved talking to her daughter but after every conversation she felt depressed because of the question her daughter repeatedly asked. Her daughter would ask: "mommy, when will you come to get me?" Rose said she dreaded that question to the point that she cut back on the calls because she always had to lie to her daughter. Yaa said that her trip back to the US after her first visit to see her husband and daughter in Ghana was so traumatic that she did not want to recall it. To make up for the guilt they felt, women increasingly sent money, at first through friends and later through money transfer agencies like Western Union. At the same time, Ghanaians have established shipping companies that have allowed for small shipments like suitcases, kitchen gadgets, and other knickknacks. Women took advantage and sent food and clothing to their children and other dependents. Some astute immigrants have opened stores in Ghana where they sell goods on credit to people whose immigrant children pay for the goods in dollars to the store owner in the US. These stores are stocked with American goods that give a sense of good living to people in Ghana who buy them.

Apart from linking up with their families, women participated in the activities of their towns by making donations to their churches during annual Christmas harvests and to bereaved families during funerals. Women who want to be dramatic would call during funeral proceedings and then have the call put on speaker so that everybody could hear them. These actions consolidate women's membership in their home communities. That consolidation was important because women intended to rejoin the communities in the future.

What we should note is that women dealt with all three levels of family concurrently. They maintained a presence in the immigrant community by attending social events when possible and making monetary contributions. They kept contact with their families in Ghana through technology and remittances. The more burdensome situation was dealing with immediate family. Immigration affected the structure of the family while women's work affected the family's internal dynamics. The reconstitution of the family and gender roles positioned women to be power brokers while also threatening the cohesion of the family as a unit. This contradiction is taken up in more detail in the next chapter.

NOTES

1. Rhacel Salazar Parrenas, "Servants of Globalization: Women, Migration and Domestic Work: Migrant Filipina Domestic Workers in Rome and Los Angeles," in *Feminist Theory Reader: Local and Global Perspectives*, ed. Carole R McCann and Seung-kyung Kim (New York: Routledge, 2013), 203.
2. Cited in Claire Renzetti, 175.
3. Renzetti.
4. Mazzucato and Kabki, "Small is Beautiful," 232; Donkor, "The Education of Immigrant Women," 157.
5. See Mazzucato and Kabki, "Small is Beautiful," 232–5.
6. See Mazzucato and Kabki, "Small is Beautiful," 234–5.
7. Parrenas, "Servants of Globalization," 205.
8. As I was concluding writing this manuscript, the government of Ghana had called a Diaspora Summit that would run for three days to get input from Ghanaians living abroad in terms of investments and other aspects of national development. This implies that not only are immigrants encouraged and expected to help family and local communities; they are now recognized at the national level as agents of change. See "Diaspora is Ghana's '11th Region,' –Government," ghanaweb, July 2, 2017, www.ghanaweb.com.
9. Anthony Giddens, *The Constitution of Society: Outline of the Theory of Structuration* (Oakland: University of California Press, 1986).
10. David Gauntlett, *Media, Gender and Identity: An Introduction* (London and New York: Routledge, 2002), http://www.theory.org.uk/gidcredit.htm.
11. Among the Akan in particular, kin fostering is common. Several situations can lead to kin fostering but the most common involves a woman who sends one or two of her children to other maternal family members to live with because of poverty. A woman who is unable to give birth can also kin-foster a niece or nephew and in time consider them as her own children.

Chapter 7

Live In at What Cost?

The preceding two chapters outlined the numerous ways in which women defined and used their agency as care workers. In the main, the women seemed to be self-assured, shattering some long-held stereotypes about private care work and offering a new, positive lens through which to gage their work. Problems of abuse and exploitation that have been endemic in discourse on domestic care work, for example, did not feature prominently in the women's work experiences. However, it would be a disservice to the women to ignore issues that they voiced, implied, or were totally silent on but were issues of major concern. While they reminisced about the hardships they suffered in Ghana that pushed them to immigrate in the first place, difficulties they encountered in transit, and their first impressions of the various Western metropolises they settled in as they slowly made their way to the US, their past difficulties did not dominate the more important issues they wanted to talk about. The most pressing of these was the dynamics in their immediate families. The women seemed to love their work but also worried that their families were getting away from them. Others worried about their children in Ghana and how soon they could reunite. Women were also concerned about the possibility of unemployment resulting from the death of a client. The women thus identified two broad interrelated areas of concern that are separated here for purposes of analysis. As they talked about their concerns, other issues that held serious long-term consequences were evident but the women did not address them. Given that this manuscript is written mostly from a historical perspective, it will seem out of place to discuss matters that are yet to happen. Yet, I feel compelled, contrary to my training and expertise, to comment on those issues as a way of drawing attention to them as serious problems that need a lot more discursive engagement.

CONCERNS WITH IMMEDIATE FAMILY

Women did not renege on their duties as mothers and wives in their families. They worked hard to keep their immediate families together; however, most expressed fears that their efforts did not seem to pay off. With regard to children, women sent money and other material things to children and their caretakers in Ghana. They also kept in close touch through letters, pictures, and phone calls. If the children were in the US, women used home visits, money, and nightly phone calls to stay in touch. What the women did not take into account was that the children, especially those in the US, would have ideas about them as mothers as they grew. Children in the US quickly Americanized through their interactions with peers in school and consumption of media. They saw soccer moms cheering their children on during games; they saw mothers taking children to amusement parks; or they saw mothers shopping with children and understood what it meant to forge a mother-child relationship. The children understood that relationships were not forged only on a material basis. Emotional and physical connections were as important as the provision of material needs. In fact, one young man who had agreed to participate in this study later pulled out because he did not know his mother well enough to talk about her. That was a startling comment from a man who grew up living with both parents. His view was that his mother was not home most of the time when he and his sister were growing up. He had grown up without a mother's care although his mother was alive and lived a few miles from their home. Thus when Hochschild and others talk of women's transfer of affection, they refer to a serious problem that only immigrant mothers and their dependent children can suffer.

Women with children felt inadequate in their inability to be there for their children like most mothers do. Rose, who sent her four-year-old daughter to Ghana, said that every time her phone rang at night her heart started. She was always afraid that a call might come from Ghana to inform her that something terrible happened to her daughter because she knew a woman who sent her child to Ghana (that woman was not a care worker) and the child died. She could not forgive herself if, in the name of work, she sent her child to Ghana only for the child to die. But that fear seemed unfounded. Many Ghanaian immigrants have sent their children to Ghana for numerous reasons and brought them back after the children had stayed in Ghana for several years without anything happening to them. The fear of a child dying appeared to be a smokescreen for a bigger problem, and that was the fear of losing the relationship with their children, in Ghana or in the US. Indeed, accounts given by the women themselves gave insights into how they believed their children related to them. Maame Esi's sons became distant as they adapted more and more to American life. Others complained of their teenage children getting out of control and threatened to send them to Ghana as punishment. Those who sent young children to Ghana worried that the children would be spoiled by their other mothers or worse, some calamity might befall them. Some, like Yaa, were concerned that they would miss their children's teenage years, while others worried that their children might have difficulty adjusting to the American education system after they had acquired a Ghanaian accent.

If women worried about their children, they also worried about their spouses. There were two areas in the marital relationship that appeared to worry the women the most. These were the men's fidelity and their use of the family money. Central to the issue of marital fidelity was how long women could stay at the workplace before they took days off. On the one hand, the men suggested that the women could come home every weekend. They implied that women's long stays were deliberate. On the other hand, the women noted that they were not paid for time off. They also worried that leaving their clients every weekend could backfire, and the clients would look for other caregivers. The majority of the women seemed to think that their significant others were cheating and there was reason for their suspicions. One of the men was blunt in his response to the charge of infidelity. He said, "I'm a man in my prime and I have needs so…" He did not end the sentence but assumed that I knew where he was going with it.

The admission of infidelity on his part was unfortunate. The women had needs too. The fact that they went home to clean and cook and make sure that their spouses were well provisioned indicated that they were well-intentioned. In fact, one of the women, Ayorkor, was convinced that her husband was cheating but did not think that it was the result of her work schedule. She indicated that before she took up her job as a caregiver, her husband worked an overnight job while she worked during the day. That arrangement worked very well for their children. They did not see each other until Saturday morning, which meant the couple spent only two days together every week. She did not use her husband's nighttime work as an excuse to cheat on him. Thus, it is safe to conclude that the men who cheated did so not because of their wives jobs (although the wives absence made the cheating easier) but because of their own personal failings as spouses. Cheating was not universal among men whose wives did live-in caregiving. It was rather the fear that it might happen that kept some of the women worrying. Ayorkor revealed the mental agony that she suffered:

> Most nights I dream myself to sleep, especially when I call and he doesn't respond. I picture his girlfriend walking about in the house. I worry that she will sleep on my part in the bed. And I certainly don't like that she might go through my things, use my pots to cook…. It's not a good place to be psychologically and emotionally when your husband is cheating on you.

Unmarried caregivers also believed that there could be infidelity in their relationships but theirs was a little bit more convoluted. Badu, for example, thought that her relationship with her boyfriend was solid. He lived with her fifteen-year-old son. When she came home on her days off they presented the picture of a family unit. They did not have joint savings but she contributed to the "family" budget. They had talked about marriage and she had told herself that she would quit her job when he proposed. Then she got a call from a woman she did not know. The caller informed Badu that she was pregnant by her boyfriend. When Badu confronted him all he said was, "well, you are not home most of the time." Stunned and confused, Badu contemplated quitting her live-in job for a day job that would enable her to be home with her son. Another woman worried that she was getting old but she was not going to be able to marry and raise a family if she was gone for months from the community. She too was thinking of going back to live-out to make it easy for her to meet someone and start a relationship.

The other area of concern to the women—possible misuse of money—led to direct and open confrontations between spouses. Nancy did not believe in joint spousal savings. She believed she must have absolute control over her money. She had plans to help her family in Ghana and having a joint account with her husband could lead to trouble if she took money for her private use. In spite of her resolve, she gave him her charge card so that he could act on her behalf if there was need for a financial transaction during her absence. Unknown to her, he had withdrawn a large sum of money from her account to repair his mother's house in Ghana. He promised to pay her back when she found out but it had taken several years and he had not made the effort. Several women said that they did not save jointly with their spouses because of issues like the one Nancy experienced. One woman, Araba, said she dreaded the thought of her husband taking money from their joint account and using it on his girlfriend (although she did not know that he had one). Gloria's house that she jointly built with her husband in Ghana as their future home had been taken over by his family. Her mother did not know that the house was a joint property and put pressure on Gloria to also build one. The problem was that her husband was not ready to help her build a house for her mother. Gloria felt cheated, but did not want to start a conflict between her family and her husband's over the house his mother lived in. The problem of one spouse appropriating a joint property in Ghana appeared to be common among Ghanaian immigrant families, not just women who did live-in. The twist for live-in workers was that it took time for them to discover that their husbands had swindled them. One woman said she stopped accepting her wages in checks and started accepting cash. She would keep the cash until her days off to make the deposit herself. Others stopped giving their bank cards to their husbands; they gave money to the men when they had to contribute to the family budget.

Concerns with Work

Live-in care work is unique from other kinds of care work in terms of the deep emotional attachment that workers and employers can develop for each other. That attachment can easily be thrown in jeopardy if something happened to the care recipient. The women in private practice indicated that one of their biggest fears was the danger of losing a client through death. Women who do live-in but work with employment agencies can always go back to the agencies to be placed with a new client when an old one passes away. Women in private practice do not have that advantage. Some are their own agent and worker at the same time. When a client passes away, they do not have automatic recourse to another client. Akua said that the death of a client was an ever-present concern that put a limit on private practice as a permanent job option. Akua, however, did not offer a timeframe within which one could conveniently retire from practice service. The problem for women here is that if they prolong their stay in private homes well into their late fifties before they quit, they may have few options in the labor market if they decide to find other jobs opportunities. In other words, staying in private practice for a long time ends up limiting women to domestic work and nothing more.

A related problem to the death of a client is the absence of counseling to alleviate women's grief and stress. The families of clients seem to have a different view of the relationships that exist between workers and clients. They seem to take such relationships strictly as work related that cease when the work ends. But that is not the case. To illustrate this we turn to Ayorkor for insights. Ayorkor had been working for the same client for twelve years. Her client was seventy-seven years old and quite healthy for his age when she started taking care of him. By the time he reached eighty-six, he was no longer able to perform very simple tasks, which meant Ayorkor's workload increased. The man complained of chest and joint pains. He also forgot easily. Ayorkor said she started praying for God to prolong her client's life so she could stay employed. For the next three years they lived day by day; several times in the month she would call emergency service and he would be rushed to the hospital, but he always came home when he was discharged instead of being in an assisted family facility, as his family suggested. Ayorkor believed that he liked coming back home because of how well she cared for him. She stopped taking her regular days off and instead went home only when he was hospitalized. Although she was not required to do so Ayorkor visited him when he had an extended admission at the hospital. She explained:

> When you live with a person for that long and you see them getting sick and weak, it does not matter that you are a worker in the house. Normal human emotions kick in and you want to help any way you can. Especially when you

> sense that they may die, you feel it is your duty to visit them and make them feel loved, although they have their own family that also come around for the same reason.

Ayorkor couched her emotional attachment to her client in familial terms. She called her client "my old man" and treated him as a grandfather. She used an analogy that drove home how she felt about death on the job. She said that taking care of a human being is not like flying on a long-distance trip. You may strike a "relationship" with the person seated next to you but once you reach your destination the relationship ends. You may remember the conversations and may even tell friends and family about a person you met on the flight, but there is something fleeting and impersonal about that kind of encounter. The same is not the case in a caregiving relationship. It may be a very long trip, and the relationship that develops is nurtured and protected. Therefore it becomes a problem when women are expected to walk away when a client dies as if they met on an airplane and the relationship did not mean anything. Thus, Ayorkor said that the most difficult part of her client's death was when she packed her things and walked out of the house that she had called her second home for twelve years. She described leaving in terms of rupture, but how soon she would have closure was her problem to deal with. At the time of her interview she had been home, unemployed, for one month but she said it was because she was not looking for a job. She would want to be in private practice again but she needed some rest. Ayorkor's story raises the question that I could not explore because I did not interview clients but it would be informative to learn from care recipients if they think care workers who are willing to participate in the funeral of a client for the sake of closure should be allowed to do so.

Women's Future Financial (In)Security

As we ponder the emotional aspect of death in a care situation, there are other issues that may not be directly related to death but that need to be exposed as areas of concern. One of these is the issue of unemployment insurance. The period that a private practice caregiver waits before she is employed again can be critical from a financial standpoint. Ordinarily, a worker will apply for unemployment insurance when she is temporarily unemployed to cushion them as they look for a new job. Home care workers in New York are no exception. The New York State Department of Labor has clear guidelines for workers who need to apply for unemployment insurance. Generally, personal service performed in private homes is covered when the employer pays the employee more than $1000 or more in a calendar quarter.[1] An employer who pays that much in wages must pay both the New York State Unemployment

Liability and the Federal Liability contributions to make it possible for the care worker to receive unemployment insurance when she is out of job. The exceptions are people who are listed as independent contractors. These are people "who are in business for themselves and [are] free from any direction and control of their work by the people who use their services."[2] Women in private practice are not independent contractors, although some negotiate the terms of their employment independently. They do not have the latitude to do their work any way they want; the clients have the final word on that. The women also receive wages above the amount stipulated by the New York Department of Labor. Therefore, they qualify to apply for and receive unemployment insurance when they lose their jobs. However, because their employers do not make the state and federal contributions—out of either ignorance or willful concealment—the women in private practice cannot apply for unemployment insurance when they lose their jobs. That means they may fall back on their savings or find something else to do immediately which may not always work out as planned. Women may experience temporary poverty or dependence when they lose their jobs.

If women's inability to collect unemployment insurance may be problematic, more serious problems concern their health and financial security in the long term. Unless they are married to people whose jobs offer health insurance that covers spouses, women have to buy their own health insurance. This issue is not unique to immigrant caregivers. There are thousands of workers, immigrant and native born, in other job sectors who do not enjoy employer covered health insurance. Such people buy private insurance. I do not know how many bought health insurance after our interviews, but none had their own health insurance. Aminata admitted that she had heard that health insurance was expensive and that one had to go through hoops to buy health insurance. She also claimed that she came home during weekends when most businesses were closed so she could not buy health insurance. While a very lame excuse, she touched on a complicated issue. Women preferred to take days off on weekends so that they would participate in community activities. Many official businesses do not open during weekends. Women could also buy insurance online, but this assumes that they had access to the internet and knew how to navigate. In the absence of health insurance, some women resorted to self-diagnosis and medication while others used emergency room services. Here is Maame Esi narrating her story about falling severely ill while on the job: "I expected my husband to take time off his job to care for me because I did not have health insurance. He also did not have health insurance and did not want to take days off work because I was already losing money by being home sick . . ."

The problem for Maame Esi and her husband was that they were investing money in a project in Ghana that limited their ability to deal with situations such as a sudden or acute illness. On the surface, one can blame the couple for misplaced priority but when we gage their behavior against the backdrop of the bridge position they occupied, it becomes clear that they were spread thin. The idea of the transnational family is not just a way for scholars to describe the fact that families are separated in the old and new countries. We draw attention to the fact that immigrant women have to spread their resources to multiple family units. It may serve the women well to focus on one issue at a time. It is nearly impossible for women to "live" in two places at the same time on an annual gross income of $20,000. However prudent they may be, there is the high possibility that they will sacrifice crucial aspects of their lives in order to make some material gains. That, I suggest, is not a winning strategy.

A serious drawback to private practice is the absence of employer-matched pension plans. Women in private practice must start their own retirement plans if they hope to live comfortably in the future. Some of the women mistook life insurance for a retirement plan. Others believed, erroneously, that they could draw on social security in the future when their employers did not make the contributions. It is up to the women to make their own contribution to be assured of a lifeline in the future. What the women probably were unaware of is that social security payments at retirement are based on credits that are determined by yearly contributions. One has to accrue 40 credits in a ten-year period to qualify for future payments.[3] The smaller the contribution during active years of work, the smaller the monthly payment at retirement. These issues are not explained to women sufficiently or at all.

An alternative for women to earn income in their old age is for them to get married and stay married into retirement. Fortunately, most of the women were married and others were contemplating marriage. Marriage, though, is only a first step. Women must be married to spouses whose jobs offer employer-matched pension schemes, and they must stay married until the spouses have reached retirement age to draw on their plans. The problem here is that there are no guarantees in such matters. Marriages break up and people die prematurely. In the latter instance, a woman can collect the deceased spouse's social security, the size of which will depend on contributions. If the couple live into retirement and then depend on only the social security payments for one person, they can face old-age poverty. There is research that shows that old-age poverty is a problem in the US but it is severer for women than it is for men. When race is factored in, Black and Hispanic women are more likely to be poorer than white women in old age.[4] Women in private practice must be made aware of these potentially serious situations so that they can make informed decisions as they continue to take care of others. Without a forward-looking plan toward their own futures, there is the likelihood that the women will face a grim financial future.

There is also the view among the women that they would resettle in Ghana in the future. The idea itself is not a bad one. After all they care for elderly people and know how much it costs to be cared for in old age in the US. If they prepare well—build a house and/or establish a business, they can relocate to Ghana and live comfortably at a fraction of what it will cost to live in the US in old age. There is no doubt that many of the women will succeed in building houses in Ghana either alone or with their spouses. It is too early to predict whether or not the women will be able to successfully relocate. What is at issue is whether future resettlement in Ghana can be guaranteed. After years of hard work and thousands of dollars in building projects and establishing businesses, women can find themselves in vulnerable situations.[5] Some borgers have lost huge sums of money because of double-dealings. Landowners can sell the same piece of land to multiple people who then engage in litigation for years or use land guards[6] to protect the plots. Infrequently a claimant to a plot will wait until an immigrant has finished building a house and then move in to claim the plot, not the house. Sometimes the problem is with renters who will not move out when it is time to do so.

Women who avoid these problems by having their projects sited in or close to their hometowns can face a different kind of challenge. One cannot build a house and then lock it up until it is time to move in when there may be family members who need a place to stay. If the immigrant makes a mistake and allows such members to move in, it will be nearly impossible to ask them to move out at a future date. To avoid such a potential problem, some build houses for their families and then another for themselves. All these require substantial outlays that may result in present sacrifices for women. As for business ownership, women who employ others to run their businesses can lose their money through corruption. At least we saw the case of Lydia whose son ran her business to the ground. When women think about the future in terms of laying a foundation in Ghana as opposed to the US, they make a gamble. If Ghana fails and there is little to rely on in the US, the future can be bleak for these women. As important as home ownership was to the women, only three owned their homes (with their spouses) in the US, although several indicated that once they had finished building their houses in Ghana, they would buy one in the US.

In spite of the attraction of private practice to the women, it carried serious short and long-term structural and familial problems that make one wonder if it is worth the women's investment in time and energy. They calculated the benefits of their work not so much against the difficulties they encountered but how much money they could make, and what that money could do in Ghana.

NOTES

1. New York Department of Labor, Unemployment Insurance Division, www.labor.ny.gov.

2. New York Department of Labor, Unemployment Insurance Division.

3. This is only based on an able-bodied worker. There are special provisions for different categories of people. For more details see Social Security Administration, https://www.ssa.gov/.

4. "Poverty among Older Women," *Family Economics and Nutrition Review* 11, no. 3 (1998): 71; Joseph F Quinn and Kevin E. Cahill, "The New World of Retirement Income Security in America," *American Psychologist* 71, no. 4 (2016): 323; "Women in America," 14.

5. In March 2017, a houseboy killed his 60-year-old homeowner at home from London to attend a friend's funeral. Some people claimed the houseboy committed the murder to take the house. See Daily Guide, "Houseboy Kills Boss at Ofankor," March 17, 2017, http://dailyguideafrica.com/houseboy-kills-boss-ofankor/.

6. Land guards are privately armed individuals who are be hired by landowners to protect their property against encroachment. They have been known to attack laborers at building sites with guns and machetes, sometimes causing death. See Ghana News Agency, "Curb Land Guard Activities in Greater Accra," April 9, 2016, https://www.modernghana.com/news/98018/curb-land-guard-activities-in-greater-accra.html.

Chapter 8

Rethinking Immigrant Women's Care Work

The stories of the women in private practice touch on theoretical and practical themes that dominate domestic care work generally. Some of the themes, captured in word pairs, have already been woven into the women's narratives. They include:

a. susceptibility vs. agency
b. exploitation vs. resilience
c. self-sacrifice vs. contentment
d. rupture vs. attachment

A cursory look at each word pair suggests that the challenges the women faced and their reactions to them did not happen in one location or as discrete experiences. They happened concurrently at different sites. When we take the first pair as an example, the women were susceptible to abuse in Ghana during the revolution; those who tried to immigrate were vulnerable to exploitation in transit; in the US they joined a work sector that was one of the least paid in the economy. Yet, they surmounted these challenges at every point until they had settled and adapted to American life. As transnational migrants, the women were caught between two worlds with vastly different relations to the global political economy. Hence, to fully comprehend their choices and responses to the conditions of care work, I used a holistic analysis that incorporated the socio-cultural and political contexts that engendered the women's migration with market conditions in the US that made live-in caregiving attractive to the women. An integrative approach allowed an intersectional analysis that utilized race, culture, gender, class, and nation. I hope that approach achieved its goal in telling the women's stories. In this concluding chapter I want to briefly examine a theoretical/philosophical perspective offered by Allison Weir on care work to determine how it bears on private practice.

I argued earlier in this book that capitalist globalization is a continuation of colonization and that both processes were built on a philosophy of exploitation and accumulation. The relatively subtle nature of exploitation and accumulation in capitalist globalization complicates the experiences of immigrants like the Ghanaian women. They were naturalized Americans whose race, color, class, and gender marked them permanently as immigrants, regardless of the number of years they had lived in the US. Their "otherness" made the exploitation of their labor acceptable. This is because immigration is considered a privilege and not a right; it would appear then that the admission of the Ghanaian women into the US and their eventual naturalization signaled a huge favor that the US did the women. Meryl Altman and Kerry Pannell describe this way of seeing immigration policy vis-à-vis public opinion of immigrants as "cognitive dissonance."[1] I want to build on their description by adding the term "patriarchal benevolence," a deliberate relaxation of immigration laws so that women who would otherwise not qualify to enter can gain admission into the US. The question is why the US would extend such a "privilege" to people who do not have the requisite qualifications, experience, and skill. Altman and Pannell provide an answer through a series of questions—"Are citizens prepared to clean their own houses, care for their own children and elderly parents, and shoulder the burden of reproductive labor on a household-by-household and day-to-day basis? And what would happen to productivity and labor force participation if they did?"[2]

Most upper and middle-class Americans will probably answer no to each of the questions because they can afford to pay low wages for the services of immigrant women of color. What appears as benevolence is only a façade. As Ehrenreich and Hochschild remind us, middle-income Americans need the release from household drudgery to be able to fully participate in the economy. That being the case, we can conclude that the admission of immigrant women of color into the US should not be perceived as either charity or compassion on women from impoverished regions of the world to improve their lives by working in the US. Given the unequal positioning of Ghana and the US in the global economy, the chance that the Ghanaian women got to enter the US was enough to blind them to the possibility that their labor could be exploited. That is exactly what capitalist globalization does; it exposes some people to its promise but not necessarily its profits. We saw that when the women talked about their work. They did not believe that they were pushed into care work. They, and I presume many others employed in the sector, did not stop to consider why there was always room in the sector for people like them. The point is that whether they are in their countries of origin or in immigrant destination countries like the US, women of color in domestic care work—caring for children, adults, the disabled, or general help—sit at the bottom rung of the economic ladder, holding it steady so that others can conveniently occupy their places in the march of capitalist globalization.

This brings me to an important theoretical perspective offered by Allison Weir in her essay "Global Care Chains." The focus of Weir's analysis is on women who care for other women's children, and thus falls outside the purview of the work of the Ghanaian women. Nonetheless, the issues she raises can be applied to private practice. Weir states that in order for us to understand care work as a "global issue, we need to begin from the perspective of the immigrant careworker" and link their background to their experiences in the immigrant destination country in order to develop a model of care with the ultimate goal of building freedom and solidarity.[3] Weir's model of care is built on the recognition that care is both a "source of freedom and responsibility, as both work and pleasure, and as both duty and desire."[4] This recognition takes into consideration the fact that there are power differences between caregivers and recipients based on race, class, and nationality, differences that appear irreconcilable but that need a feminist rethinking in order for the freedom and solidarity she envisions to occur. Hence, Weir constructs a well-grounded three-point principle that, if put into practice, will recognize the power differences between women not in oppositional terms but in terms of interdependence. She asks for fair wages and social support for care work, equitable distribution of care and a view of care as an "intrinsic good, a source of identity and meaning, that should be recognized as a human right."[5] The right to give and receive care should be recognized as a core component of our lives as social beings, hence the allusion to care as a human right.

Individual choice or agency is at the heart of the freedom Weir envisions. If women are not forced to choose from options in situations that put them in a bind, they will have the capacity to decide what they want to do and on what terms. For instance, women would not have to make the difficult decision to leave their children behind in order to migrate. Weir draws on the ideas of scholars like Chandra Mohanty, Patricia Hill Collins, Cynthia Willet, and Sherene Razack to invoke an expansive view of freedom and solidarity that recognizes differences among women as well as women's oppression that is not based on a single factor but produced through an interlocking system. Seen this way, women can acknowledge their differences while also embracing their interdependence as a basis for solidarity. This vision of freedom for women should not be restricted to only immigrant women but to women globally, on the premise that care must be prioritized as a social good and responsibility that must be paid for by the public.[6]

Applied to the Ghanaian women, the concept of freedom as interdependence, as mutual recognition of the worth of both the caregiver and care recipient helps to explain why the kinds of vulnerabilities that have been reported in other care relationships were almost absent. However, when we place the women's experience of care within the context of globalization, the practical aspect of both freedom and solidarity becomes complicated. Like most Third World countries, the hardships that the women experienced in Ghana reflected the accumulated effects of colonialism, imperialism, neo-colonialism, globalization, and local cultural practices. Therefore when the women migrated, it was not the result of free choice; they were forced. On the surface, it would appear that the women made conscious decisions to migrate; however, the contexts in which they embarked on migration did not lend themselves to a perception of free choice even if the women's decisions to migrate were deliberate. I make these statements cognizant of the fact that Weir was looking ahead into the future when she proposed those principles. My point is that decades of foreign impositions and exploitation have created volatile conditions in countries like Ghana to a degree that individual decisions to migrate now or in the future cannot be made from a position of freedom of choice. Regarding solidarity, women in private practice generally did not take care of women, thus the chance for bonding with their employers as a feminist gesture of female solidarity was simply not possible.

As a theoretical perspective, Weir's "Global Care Chains" holds the promise of not only freedom for and solidarity among women; it also promises peace, justice, and fairness in society at large. If, as she states, care can be distributed so that women are not unduly saddled—if care will be recognized as social responsibility, valued as a public good, seen as a human right and remunerated accordingly—then society as a whole will be the better for it. Nonetheless, the practical application of this vision in the global political economy may be problematic. There should be social and cultural reform for people to begin to value care, bearing in mind that certain cultural and social beliefs and practices may be impervious to change. We don't know yet if men and upper and middle-class women will, in the name of freedom and solidarity, give up their privilege and help to reverse "pass on," that is, men relinquishing domestic work to women who in turn pass it on to poorer women.[7] If change at the individual, micro level may be difficult to achieve, it is going to be more difficult still to achieve change at the global, macro level with capitalism dominating economies. Capitalism engenders power for countries that control larger portions of global resources. If Third World women work to sustain Frist World wealth and power, it will take a high level of altruism for wealthy nations to release these women from their poverty by remunerating care work handsomely. It is not even clear if public funding of care in all its diversity is feasible. In the case of private practice, individual men who are old but not necessarily sick employ the services of women. How these men join the conversation on care so that the women who care for them, many of them American citizens, will be treated like other care workers is another problematic that the theory does not adequately resolve. A silver lining is the projected increase in the senior population and negative view about immigrants in the country. If immigrant intake is reduced in the coming years and other factors remain the same, demand for care workers will outstrip supply and push its value in terms of remuneration.

Moving away from the theoretical consideration to practical matters, the Ghanaian women's stories reveal the need for some of the key problems associated with care work to be examined in context. For instance, the problem of invisibility had a different meaning for the women in private practice than what scholars and other experts emphasize as a matter of concern. Experts have emphasized that women's invisibility as workers in private homes exposes women to abuse. Invisibility also leads to a lack of recognition of care work as real work. And if private care work is not real work, then it cannot be governed by the same labor laws that govern other work sectors in the country. This is a serious issue that should concern all private care workers. The Ghanaian women also had to deal with invisibility in the Ghanaian immigrant community. Their work in private homes potentially hurt their community membership, participation, and benefits. As immigrants, they stood to gain by participating in the community; whatever benefits they hoped to gain seemed to trump other questions regarding invisibility outside of the Ghanaian immigrant community.

The women downplayed the problem of abuse and exploitation in their work relations because of a thought process that I called regressive thinking. If they lived in rural communities, as exemplified by Aminata, they did physically demanding labor. Compared with what they did in Ghana, private care was not work to complain about. Until fairly recently, most rural communities did not have potable water. Women woke up at dawn, some as early as 4 a.m., to fetch water. They also walked long distances to get firewood. Now in the US they enjoy uninterrupted water supply; they don't boil water to bathe or use for other household needs; they don't chop wood or burn newspaper to start a fire when they want to cook; they don't worry that there will be power outage to interrupt the day's activities; and they don't bend to sweep—simply, domestic work in the US is easy compared with domestic work in Ghana.

The same kind of "thinking back" characterized remuneration. All a woman had to do was to know the prevailing exchange rate and they had an idea how much they were making in Ghanaian cedis. Lest we begin to question the women's intelligence, we should note that they did not intend to spend their earnings in the US. Therefore it made perfect sense for them to make that mental conversion and end up believing that they were paid well. Taken together as a package, if the women did not feel abused or exploited, and believed that they were paid well, then they had reason to believe that their type of private care work was of a higher quality than the rest. And if that was what they believed, can we say they were wrong?

NOTES

1. Altman and Pannell, "Policy Gaps and Theory Gaps," 296.
2. Altman and Pannell, "Policy Gaps and Theory Gaps, 296.
3. Weir, "Global Care Chains," 166–7.
4. Weir, "Global Care Chains," 167.
5. Weir, "Global Care Chains," 167.
6. Weir, "Global Care Chains," 169.
7. Weir, "Global Care Chains," 172; Hochschild, "Love and Gold," in *Global Woman: Nannies, Maids, Sex Workers and the New Economy,* eds. Barbara Ehrenreich and Arlie Russell Hochschild (New York: Metropolitan Books, 2002), 19.

Bibliography

Abdulai, Abdul-Gafaru. "Political Context Study—Ghana." Human Rights, Power and Civic Action Research Project, Universities of Oslo, Leeds and Ghana, January 2009. http://www.polis.leeds.ac.uk/assets/files/research/research-projects/abdulai-ghana-political-context-study-jan09.pdf.

Accra Mail. "We are not Savages—Chief Nana Kwa Bonko V." Ghanaweb.com, January 19, 2003. http://www.ghanaweb.com/GhanaHomePage/NewsArchive/We-Are-Not-Savages-Chief-Nana-Kwa-Bonko-V-31766.

Adepoju, Aderanti. "Migration in Africa: An Overview." In *The Migration Experience in Africa,* edited by Jonathan Baker and Tade Akin Aina, 87–108. Sweden: Nordiska Afrikainstitutet, 1995.

———. "The Demographic Profile: Sustained High Mortality, Fertility and Migration for Employment." In *Gender, Work and Population in Sub-Saharan Africa,* edited by Christine Oppong and Aderanti Adepoju, 17–34. London: James Currie Ltd, 1994.

Afolayan, Funso. "Kingdoms of West Africa: Benin, Oyo, and Asante." In *African History before 1885,* edited by Toyin Falola, 161–189. Durham, NC: Carolina Academic Press, 2003.

Ahiakpor, James C. W. "Multinational Corporations in the Third World: Predators or Allies in Economic Development? *Religion and Liberty* 2, no. 5 (September and October 1992). http://www.acton.org/pub/religion-liberty/volume-2-number-5/multinational-corporations-third-world-predators-o.

Akurang-Parry, Kwabena O. "Aspects of Elite Women's Activism in the Gold Coast, 1874–1890." *International Journal of African Historical Studies* 37, no. 3 (2004): 463–482.

Allah-Mensah, Beatrix. *Women in Politics and Public Life in Ghana.* Accra: Friedrich-Ebert Foundation, 2005.

Altman, Meryl, and Kerry Pannell. "Policy Gaps and Theory Gaps: Women and Migrant Domestic Labor." *Feminist Economics* 18, no. 2 (April 2012): 291–315. DOI: http://dx.doi.org/10.1080/13545701.2012.704149.

Ambrosini, Maurizio. "Inside the Invisible Welfare: Helping Immigrant Domestic Workers and Caregivers to the Elderly." *Studi Emigrazione/Migration Studies* 42, no. 159 (2005): 561–595.

American Community Survey. Place of Birth by Citizenship Status, 2006–2010. American Community Survey Selected Population Tables. https://factfinder.census.gov/faces/tableservices/jsf/pages/productview.xhtml?pid=ACS_10_SF4_B05002&prodType=table.

Anderson, Margaret, and Dana Hysock. *Thinking about Women: Sociological Perspectives on Sex and Gender.* Boston: Allyn and Bacon, 2009.

Aremu, Johnson Olaosebikan. "Responses to the 1983 Expulsion of Aliens from Nigeria: A Critic." *African Research Review* 7, no. 3 (July 2013): 340–352. http://dx.doi.org/10.4314/afrrev.v7i3.24.

Armstrong, Pat, and Hugh Armstrong. "Thinking Globally: Women, Work and Caring." In *Women in a Globalizing World: Transforming Equality, Development, Diversity and Peace*, edited by Angela Miles, 77–87. Toronto: Inanna Publications and Education Inc., 2013.

Arthur, John A. *African Women Immigrants in the United States: Crossing Transnational Borders.* New York: Palgrave McMillan, 2009.

Auerbach, Debra. "Best Bets for Jobs in 2012." Career Builder, January 2, 2012. http://www.CareerBuilder.com.

"Autograph on Joy Prime: Nathaniel Attoh interviews Hon. Kennedy Agyapong." https://www.youtube.com/watch?v=JlMKjGsf2P8.

Awumbila, Mariama, Joseph Teye and Joseph Yaro. "Gendered Dynamics of Migrant Domestic Work in Accra, Ghana." Legon, Accra: Centre for Migration Studies, University of Ghana, 2015. https://www.slideshare.net/MOOPCOMMS/gendered-dynamics-of-migrant-domestic-work-in-accra-ghana.

Bajaj, Vikas. "Fatal Fire in Bangladesh Highlights the Dangers Facing Garment Workers." *New York Times*, November 25, 2012. http://www.nytimes.com/2012/11/26/world/asia/bangladesh-fire-kills-more-than-100-and-injures-many.html?_r=0.

Bakan, Abigail, and Daiva Stasiulis. *Negotiating Citizenship: Migrant Women in Canada and the Global System.* Toronto: University of Toronto Press, 2005.

Bentsi-Enchill, Nii K. "Shaping a Revolution." *West Africa.* January 3 (1983): 5–7.

———. "Ghana Absorbs its Own." *West Africa.* February 14 (1983): 382–385.

Blakely, Allison. *Blacks in the Dutch World: The Evolution of Racial Imagery in a Modern Society.* Bloomington: Indiana University Press, 1993.

Bleek, Wolf. "Family and Family Planning in Southern Ghana." In *Sex Roles, Population and Development in West Africa,* edited by Christine Oppong, 138–153. London: James Currie, 1987.

Boafo-Arthur, Kwame. "A Decade of Liberalism in Perspective." In *Ghana: One Decade of the Liberal State*, edited by Kwame Boafo-Arthur, 1–20. London: Zed Books, 2007.

Bonato, Stefani, and McKenna Coll. "Domestic Workers' Rights in the United States." A report prepared for the U.N. Human Rights Committee in response to the Second and Third Periodic Report of the United States, n.d.

Booven, Valerie Van. "Joplin, Missouri Home Care Aide Accused of Stealing from Client's Debit Card." HomeCareDaily.com. https://www.homecaredaily.com/2015/12/06/missouri-home-care-aide-accused-of-stealing-from-clients-debit-card/.

Boris, Eileen, and Jennifer Klein. *Caring for America: Home Health Workers in the Shadow of the Welfare State*. New York: Oxford University Press, 2012.

Boserup, Ester. *Woman's Role in Economic Development*. London: George Allen and Unwin, 1970.

Bowers, Lois A. "Assisted Living Resident Allegedly Raped." *Springfield News-Leader*, April 2, 2017. http://www.bing.com/search?q=seniors+in+assisted+living+facilities+raped&src=IE-SearchBox&FORM=IESR02.

Boyd, Monica, and Elizabeth Grieco. "Women and Migration: Incorporating Gender into International Migration Theory." Migration Policy Institute, March 1, 2003. http://www.migrationpolicy.org/article/women-and-migration-incorporating-gender-international-migration-theory/.

Brands, H.W, T. H. Breen, R. Hal Williams, and Ariela J. Gross. *American Stories: A History of the United States*. Upper Saddle River, NJ: Pearson, 2015.

Branigin, William, and Douglas Farah. "Asylum Seeker is Imposter, INS Says." *Washington Post*, December 2000, posted with permission by the University of Maryland. http://jclass.umd.edu/archive/newshoax/casestudies/idfraud/IDAsylum3.html.

Brydon, Lynne. "The Dimensions of Subordination: A Case Study from Avatime." In *Women, Work and Ideology*, edited by Haleh Afshar, 108–127. London and New York: Tavistock Publishing, 1985.

Bump, Micah. "Ghana: Searching for Opportunities at Home and Abroad." Migration Policy Institute, March 1, 2006. http://www.migrationpolicy.org/article/ghana-searching-opportunities-home-and-abroad/.

Byrd, Nancy Zarate. "The Dirty Side of Domestic Work: An Underground economy and the Exploitation of Undocumented Workers." *DePaul Journal for Social Justice* 3, no. 2 (Spring 2010): 245–276. http://via.library.depaul.edu/jsj/vol3/iss2/6.

Carens, Joseph. "Aliens and Citizens: The Case for Open Borders." *The Review of Politics* 49, no. 2 (1987): 251–273.

CBS News. "Growing Old, Baby Boomer Style," January 10, 2006. http://www.cbsnews.com/news/growing-old-baby-boomer-style/.

Choudry, Aziz, and Hlatshwayo Mondli. *Just Work? Migrant Workers' Struggles Today*. Wildcat: Pluto Press, 2015.

Coe, Cati. "What is Love? The Materiality of Care in Ghanaian Transnational Families." *International Migration* 49, no. 6 (2011): 7–24.

Corra, Mamadi K., and Sitawa R Kimuna. "Double Jeopardy? Female African and Caribbean Immigrants in the United States." *Journal of Ethnic and Migration Studies* 35, no. 6 (July 2009): 1015–1035.

"Culture, Gender and Development." Report submitted to the African Institute for Economic Development and Planning (IDEP). The Centre for Gender and Social Policy Studies, Obafemi Awolowo University, Ile-Ife, Nigeria, Dakar, Senegal, October 2001.

Daily Guide. "Houseboy Kills Boss at Ofankor." March 17, 2017. http://dailyguideafrica.com/houseboy-kills-boss-ofankor/.

Dalla Costa, Mariarosa. "A General Strike." In *All Work and No Pay: Women, Housework, and the Wages Due*, edited by Wendy Edmond and Suzie Fleming, 125–127. London: Power of Women Collective and Falling Wall Press, 1975.

Dasgupta, Monisha. "Housework, Feminism, and Labor Activism: Lessons from Domestic Workers in New York." *Signs: Journal of Women in Culture and Society* 33, no. 3 (2008): 532–537.

Davidson, Basil. *Modern Africa: A Social and Political History*. Harlow: Longman, 1994.

Department of Homeland Security. Immigration Data and Statistics. Refugees and Asylees Data Tables, Refugee Arrivals into the United States by Region and Country of Chargeability. Fiscal Years 1990–2004.

———. *Yearbook of Immigration Statistics*, Washington, DC: Office of Immigration Statistics, 1986–1992.

———. *Yearbook of Immigration Statistics*, Washington, DC: Office of Immigration Statistics 1979–1985.

Deshingkar, Priya, and Benjamin Zeitlyn. "South-South Migration for Domestic Work and Poverty." *Geography Compass* 9, no. 4 (2015): 169–179. DOI 10.1111/gec3.12200.

"Diaspora is Ghana's '11th Region,' –Government." ghanaweb, July 2, 2017. www.ghanaweb.com.

"Domestic Workers' Rights in the United States." A Report Prepared for the U. N. Human Rights Committee in Response to the Second and Third Periodic Reports of the United States. http://www.law.unc.edu/documents/clinicalprograms/domesticworkersreport.pdf.

Donkor, Martha. "I'm Divorcing Because I Drank Lake Ontario: Marital Breakdown in Ghanaian Immigrant Families in Toronto." *Southern Journal of Canadian Studies* 5, nos. 1–2 (December 2012): 239–252.

———. *Sudanese Refugees in the United States: The Collateral Damage of Sudan's Civil War.* Lewiston, NY: The Edwin Mellen Press, 2008.

———. "Marching to the Tune: Colonization, Globalization, Immigration and the Ghanaian Diaspora." *Africa Today* 52, no. 1 (Fall 2005): 27–44.

———. "Looking Back and Looking In: Re-thinking Adaptation Strategies of Ghanaian Immigrant Women in Canada." *Journal of International Migration and Integration*, 5 no. 1 (Winter 2004): 33–51.

———. "The Education of Immigrant Women: Prospects and Challenges for Ghanaian Immigrant Women in Canada." PhD diss., Ontario Institute for Studies in Education, University of Toronto, 2000.

Edmond, Wendy, and Suzie Fleming. "If Women were Paid for all They Do." In *All Work and No Pay: Women, Housework, and the Wages Due*, edited by Wendy Edmond and Suzie Fleming, 5–12. London: Power of Women Collective and Falling Wall Press, 1975.

Ehrenreich, Barbara, and Arlie R. Hochschild, eds. *Global Woman: Nannies, Maids and Sex Workers in the New Economy*. New York: Holt Paperbacks, 2002.

Employment and Immigration Canada. *Immigration Statistics,* 1979–1985; 1986–1992.

Essed, Philomena. *Diversity: Gender, Colour and Culture*. Amherst: University of Massachusetts Press, 1996.

Everett, Jana, and Sue Ellen M. Charlton. *Women Navigating Globalization: Feminist Approaches to Development*. Lanham: Rowman and Littlefield, 2014.

Flores-Gonzalez, Nilda, Anna Romina Guevarra, Maura Toro-Morn, and Grace Chang, eds. *Immigrant Women Workers in the Neoliberal Age*. Urbana: University of Illinois 2013.

Foner, Nancy. *Across Generations: Immigrant Families in America*. New York: New York University Press, 2009.

Foner, Nancy, and George M. Fredrickson, eds. *Not Just Black and White: Historical and Contemporary Perspectives on Immigration, Race and Ethnicity in the United States*, New York: Russell Sage Foundation, 2004.

"Former President Mahama builds multi-million cedi mansion in Bole." Ghanaweb, May 19, 2017. http:// www.ghanaweb.com.

Fraser, Nancy. "After the Family Wage: A Postindustrial Thought Experiment." In *Justice Interruptus: Critical Reflection on the "Postsocialist" Condition*. New York and London: Routledge, 1997.

Frimpong-Ansah, Jonathan H. *The Vampire State in Africa: The Political Economy of Decline in Ghana*. London: James Currie Ltd, 1993.

Frye, Marilyn. *The Politics of Reality: Essays in Feminist Theory*. Trumansburg, NY: The Crossing Press, 1983.

Garey, Anita Ilta, and Karen V. Hansen, eds. *At the Heart of Work and Family: Engaging the Ideas of Arlie Hochschild*. New Jersey: Rutgers University Press, 2015.

Gauntlett, David. *Media, Gender and Identity: An Introduction*. London and New York: Routledge, 2002. http://www.theory.org.uk/gidcredit.htm.

Getz, Trevor R., and Liz Clarke. *Abina and the Important Men: A Graphic History*. New York: Oxford University Press, 2011.

Ghana News Agency. "Curb Land Guard Activities in Greater Accra." April 9, 2016. https://www.modernghana.com/news/98018/curb-land-guard-activities-in-greater-accra.html.

Giddens, Anthony. *The Constitution of Society: Outline of the Theory of Structuration*. Oakland: University of California Press, 1986.

Giddings, Paula. *When and Where I Enter: The Impact of Black Women on Race and Sex in America*. New York: Bantam Books, 1984.

Glenn, Evelyn Nakano. "From Servitude to Service Work: Historical Continuities in the Racial Division of Paid Reproductive Labour." *Signs: A Journal of Women in Culture and Society* 18, no. 1 (Autumn 1992): 1–43.

———. "Creating a Caring Society." *Contemporary Sociology* 29, no. 1 (Jan 2000): 84–94.

Government of Ghana. "Parliament of Ghana." http://www.parliament.gh/mps?leadership.

Grace, Francie. "Mutilation Horror, or Hoax?" *CBS News*, January 14, 2003. http://www.cbsnews.com/news/mutilation-horror-or-hoax/.

Gray, Natasha. "Witches, Oracles, and Colonial Law: Evolving Anti-Witchcraft Practices in Ghana, 1927–1932." *The International Journal of African Historical Studies* 34, no.2 (2001): 339–363.

Greenberg, Mark. "New Steps for Federal Child Care Policy," *The Future of Children* 17, no. 2 (Fall 2007): 73–96.

Gugler, Joseph, and Gudrun Ludwar-Ene, "Gender and Migration in Africa South of the Sahara." In *The Migration Experience in Africa*, edited by Jonathan Baker and Tade Akin Aina, 257–268. Upsala: Nordiska Afrikainstitutet, 1995.

Harley, Sharon. *Women's Labor in the Global Economy: Speaking in Multiple Voices*. New Brunswick, NJ: Rutgers University Press, 2007.

Hart, Beth. "How Shehu Shagari Expelled a Million Ghanaians from Nigeria." https://www.naij.com/575451-photos-shehu-shagari-expelled-million-nigeria-consequences.html.

Hartmann, Heidi. "The Unhappy Marriage of Marxism and Feminism: Toward a More Progressive Union." In *Feminist Theory Reader: Local and Global Perspectives,* edited by Carole R. McCann and Seung-Kyung Kim, 187–201. New York: Routledge, 2013.

Hawkins, Freda. *The Asylum Seekers.* Toronto: Canadian Institute of International Affairs, 1994.

Held, David, and Paul Hirst. "Globalization: The Argument of Our Time," *Open Democracy*, 2002. http://www.opendemocracy.com.

Henshall Momsen, Janet. *Gender, Migration and Domestic Service.* Routledge International Studies of Women and Place. Hoboken: Taylor and Francis, 1999.

Herbst, Jeffery. *The Politics of Reform in Ghana, 1982–1992.* Berkeley: University of California Press, 1993.

Hochschild, Arlie Russell. *The Time Bind: When Work becomes Home and Home becomes Work.* New York: Holt Paperbacks, 1997.

———. *The Second Shift: Working Families and the Revolution at Home*. New York: Penguin Books, 2009.

———. "Love and Gold." In *Global Woman: Nannies, Maids, Sex Workers and the New Economy,* edited by Barbara Ehrenreich and Arlie Russell Hochschild, 15–30. New York: Metropolitan Books, 2002.

———. "Global Care Chains and Emotional Surplus Value." In *On the Edge: Living with Global Capitalism,* edited by Anthony Giddens and Will Hutton, 130–146. London: Vintage Press, 2001.

Hondagneu-Sotelo, Pierrette. "Blowups and Other Unhappy Endings." In *Global Woman: Nannies, Maid, and Sex Workers in the New Economy,* edited by Barbara Ehrenreich and Arlie R. Hochschild , 55–69. New York: Metropolitan Books, 2002.

———. *Doméstica Immigrant Workers Cleaning and Caring in the Shadows of Affluence*, 2nd ed. Berkeley: University of California Press, 2007.

———. "Latina Immigrant Domestic Workers: Pathways for Cleaning and Caring Jobs." *A Journal of Chicano Studies* 26, no. 2 (fall 2001): 174–181.

Hondagneu-Sotelo, Pierrette, and Ernestine Avila. ""I'm Here, but I'm There": The Meanings of Latina Transnational Motherhood." *Gender and Society* 11, no. 5 (1997): 548–571.

Huang, Shirlena, Brenda S. A. Yeoh and Mika Toyota. "Caring for the Elderly: The Embodied Labour of Migrant Care Workers in Singapore." *Global Networks* 12, no. 2 (2012): 195–215.

Human Rights Watch. "Hidden in the Home: Abuse of Domestic Workers with Special Visas in the United States," 13, no. 2 (G) (June 2001): 1–54.

———. "Maid to Order: Ending Abuses against Migrant Domestic Workers in Singapore," Dec 6, 2005. https://www.hrw.org/report/2005/12/06/maid-order/ending-abuses-against-migrant-domestic-workers-singapore.

Hunter, Tera. "Domination and Resistance: The Politics of Wage Household Labor in New South Atlanta." In *We Specialize in the Wholly Impossible: A Reader in Black Women's History*, edited by Darlene Clark Hine, Wilma Kin and Linda Reed, 343–357. Brooklyn, NY: Carlson Publishing, Inc., 1995.

Hutter, Mark. "My Filipina is from Ghana: Transnational Migration, Nannies and Family Life." *Journal of Comparative Family Studies* 44, no. 6 (Nov/Dec 2013): 741–748.

Hyden, Goran. *Beyond Ujamaa in Tanzania: Underdevelopment and an Uncaptured Peasantry*. Berkeley: University of California Press 1980.

Imoh, Afua-Twum Boafo. "Searching for a Middle Ground in Children's Rights in Ghana." *Journal of Human Rights* 10 (2011): 376–392. DOI: 10.1080/14754835.2011.596067.

International Labour Organization. *Domestic Workers across the World: Global and Regional Statistics and the Extent of Legal Protection*. Geneva: International Labour Organization, 2013.

Irving, Zoe. "Transformation and Persistence in the Gender Division of Labor." In *Introducing Gender and Women's Studies*, edited by Victoria Robinson and Diane Richardson, 206–229. London: Palgrave, 2015.

Isaksen, L. W. "Gender and Care: The Role of Cultural Ideas of Dirt and Disgust.' In *Gender, Bodies and Work*, edited by D. Morgan, B. Brandth and E. Kvande, 115–126. Aldershot: Ashgate, 2005.

Kasozi, A.B.K. *The Integration of Black African Immigrants in Canadian Society: A Case Study of Toronto CMA*. Toronto: Canadian African Newcomer Aid Centre of Toronto: 1986.

———. *Enabling African Immigrants Access Services: The Search for a Working Service Delivery Model*. North York, ON: African Training and Employment Centre, 1993.

Kerr, Gordon. *Short History of Africa: From the Origins of Human History to the Arab Spring*. Herpenden: Oldcastle Book, 2012. E-Book.

Kiely, Ray. "Poverty Reduction through Liberalisation? Neoliberalism and the Myth of Global Convergence." *Review of International Studies* 33, no. 3 (2007): 415–435.

Kittay, Eva Feder. "The Global Heart Transplant and Caring across National Boundaries." *The Southern Journal of Philosophy* 46 (2008): 138–165.

Kiwekete, H. "Women and the Psychosocial Hazards They Face at Work—The Plight of Immigrant Female Domestic Workers of African Origin." *African Newsletter on Occupational Health and Safety* 18, no. 3 (2008): 52–53.

Knutsen, Hege. "Globalisation and the Garment Industry in Sri Lanka." *Journal of Contemporary Asia* 33, no. 3 (2003): 225–250.

Kochanek, Kenneth D., Sherry L. Murphy, Jiaquan Xu and Betzaida Tejada-Vera. "Deaths: Final Data for 2014." *National Vital Statistics Report* 65, no. 4, June 30, 2016. https://www.cdc.gov/nchs/fastats/life-expectancy.htm.

Konadu-Agyemang, Kwadwo. "The Best of Times and the Worst of Times: Structural Adjustment Programs and Uneven Development in Africa: The Case of Ghana." *Professional Geographer* 52, no. 3 (2000): 469–483.

Kposowa, Augustine J. "*Human* Capital and the Performance of African Immigrants in the U.S. Labor Market." *The Western Journal of Black Studies* 26, no. 3 (2002): 175–183.

Kuwait Times. "Filipina Maid Dies in Botched Escape." *Kuwait Times*, March 21, 2017. http://news.kuwaittimes.net/filipina-maid-dies-in-botched-escape/.

Laurent, Olivier. "Haiti Earthquake: Five Years After." *Time*, January 2, 2015. http://time.com/3662225/haiti-earthquake-five-year-after/.

Lutz, Helma. *The New Maids: Transnational Women and the Care Economy*. London: Zed Books, 2011.

Martin, Linda, and Kerry Segrave. *The Servant Problem: Domestics Workers in North America*. Jefferson, NC: McFarland, 1985.

Mata, Irene. *Domestic Disturbances Re-Imagining Narratives of Gender, Labor, and Immigration*. Austin: University of Texas Press, 2014.

Mattei, Rudy P. "Economic I: Pull Factors." *Encyclopedia of American Immigration* (2001): 257–264.

Mattingly, Doreen J. "The Home and the World: Domestic Service and International Networks of Caring Labor." *Annals of the Association of American Geographers* 91, no. 2 (2001): 370–386.

May, Vanessa H. *Unprotected Labor Household Workers, Politics, and Middle-Class Reform in New York, 1879–1940*. Chapel Hill, NC: University of North Carolina Press, 2011.

May-Rivas, Lynn. "Invisible Labors: Caring for the Independent Person." In *Global Woman: Nannies, Maid, and Sex Workers in the New Economy*, edited by Barbara Ehrenreich and Arlie R. Hochschild, 70–84. New York: Metropolitan Books, 2002.

———. "Invisible Care and the Illusion of Independence." In *At the Heart of Work and Family: Engaging the Ideas of Arlie Hochschild*, edited by Anita Ilta Garey and Karen V. Hansen, 180–190. New Jersey: Rutgers University Press, 2015.

Mazzucato, Valentina. "The Double Engagement: Transnationalism and Integration. Ghanaian Migrants' Lives between Ghana and the Netherlands." *Journal of Ethnic and Migration Studies* 34, no. 2 (March 2008): 199–216.

Mazzucato, Valentina, and Mirjam Kabki. "Small is Beautiful: The Micro-politics of Transnational Relationships between Ghanaian Hometown Associations and Communities Back Home." *Global Networks* 9, no. 2 (2009): 227–251.

McCaskie, T. C. "The Life and Afterlife of Yaa Asantewaa." *Africa* 77, no. 2 (2007): 151–179.

Mendoza, Breny. "Transnational Feminism in Question." *Feminist Theory* 3, no. 3 (2002): 313–332.

Meredith, Robyn, and Suzanne Hoppough. "Why Globalization is Good." reprinted In *Taking Sides: Clashing Views on Global Issues,* edited by James E Harf and Michael O. Lombardi, 259–262. New York: McGraw-Hill, 2010.

Meredith, Sam. "US Life Expectancy is Low and is now projected to be on Par with Mexico by 2030." CNBC, Wednesday, February 22, 2017. http://www.cnbc.com/2017/02/22/us-life-expectancy-is-low-and-is-now-projected-to-be-on-par-with-mexico-by-2030.html.

Mfum-Mensah, Obed. *Education, Social Progress, and Marginalized Children in Sub-Saharan Africa: Historical Antecedents and Contemporary Challenges.* Lanham: Lexington Books, 2017.

Mikell, Gwendolyn. 'Ghanaian Females, Rural Economy and National Stability. *African Studies Review* 29, no. 3 (September 1986): 67–88.

Ministry of Education. n.d. "Data for the School Year 2007/2008." https://www.unicef.org/wcaro/wcaro_GHA_MTSP2.pdf.

Misra, Joya, Jennifer Hickes Lundquist and Abby Templer. "Gender, Work Time, and Care Responsibilities among Faculty." *Sociological Forum* 27, no. 2 (June 2012): 300–323.

Mohanty, Chadra Talpade. "Under Western Eyes: Feminist Scholarship and Colonial Discourses." *Boundary 2*, 12, no. 3 (Spring—Autumn, 1984): 333–358.

Mosco, Steve. "Aide Stole $800,000 from Elderly Patient." *Times Ledger*, May 11, 2012. http://www.timesledger.com/stories/2012/19/homehealthaide_fh_2012_05_10_q.html.

Nadasen, Premilla. "Citizenship Rights, Domestic Work, and the Fair Labor Standards Act." *The Journal of Policy History* 24, no. 1 (2012): 74–94. DOI: 10.1017/S0898030611000388.

Newcomb, Alyssa. "Washington Couple could face Decades in Prison for Adopted Daughter's Death." ABC News, September 10, 2013. http://abcnews.go.com/US/washington-couple-face-decades-prison-death-adopted-daughter/story?id=20216426.

New York Department of Labor. Unemployment Insurance Division. www.labor.ny.gov.

Nilliasca, Terri. "Some Women's Work: Domestic Work, Class, Race, Heteropatriarchy, and the Limits of Legal Reform." *Michigan Journal of Race & Law* 16 (2011): 377–439.

O'Barr, Jean, and Kathryn Fimin-Sellers. "African Women in Politics," In *African Women South of the Sahara*, edited by Margaret Jean Hay and Sharon Stichter, 189–212. New York: John Wiley and Sons, 1995.

Ocran, A. K. *Politics of the Sword: A Personal Memoir on Military Involvement in Ghana and the Problems of Military Government.* London: Rex Colins Limited, 1977.

Odei-Akuffo, Felix. "Teenage Pregnancies and School Dropouts: The Relevance of Family Life Education and Vocational Training to Girls Employment Opportunities." In *Sex Roles, Population and Development in West Africa,* edited by Christine Oppong, 154–164. London: James Currie, 1987.

Onimode, Bade. *The IMF, the World Bank and the African Debt: The Economic Impact.* London and New Jersey: Zed Books, 1989.

Opoku-Acheampong, Kwesi. "The Ghanaian Way of Life in Lagos." *West Africa*, January 24 (1983): 213–214.

Opoku-Dapaah, Edward. "Ghana 1981–1991: A Decade of Forced repression and Migration." *Refuge* 11, no. 3 (1992): 8–13.

———. *Adaptation of Ghanaian Immigrants in Toronto*. North York: York Lanes Press, 1993.

Panapress. "Ghanaians abroad send back home up to a billion." http://www.panapress.com/Ghanaians-abroad-send-back-home-up-to-a-billion-dollars--12-554915-72-lang4-index.html.

Parekh, Serena. "Care and Human Rights in a Globalized World." *The Southern Journal of Philosophy* 46 (2008): 104–110.

Parreñas, Rhacel Salazar. *"Servants of Globalization: Women, Migration and Domestic Work: Migrant Filipina Domestic Workers in Role and Los Angeles."* In *Feminist Theory Reader: Local and Global Perspectives*, edited by Carole R. McCann and Seung-kyun Kim, 202–217. New York: Routledge, 2013.

———. "The Care Crisis in the Philippines: Children and Transnational Families in the New Global Economy." In *Global Woman: Nannies, Maids, Sex Workers and the New Economy,* edited by Barbara Ehrenreich and Arlie Russell Hochschild, 39–54. New York: Metropolitan Books, 2002.

Parliament of Ghana. http://www.parliament.gh/mps?leadership.

"Pathways of Women's Empowerment." February 11, 2008. http://pathwaysghana.blogspot.com/2008/02/womens-participation-in-politics-in.html.

Pereira, Sónia. "Replacement Migration and Changing Preferences: Immigrant Workers in Cleaning and Domestic Service in Portugal." *Journal of Ethnic and Migration Studies* 39, no. 7 (2013): 1141–1158.

Pellow Deborah, and Naomi Chazan. *Ghana: Coping with Uncertainty*. Boulder, CO.: Westview Press, 1986.

Peterson, V. Spike, and Anne Sisson Runyan. *Global Gender Issues in the New Millennium*. Boulder, CO: Westview Press, 2010.

Perkins-Valdez, Dolen. *Wench*. New York: HarperCollins, 2010.

"Poverty among Older Women," *Family Economics and Nutrition Review* 11, no. 3 (1998): 71–73.

Pratt, Geraldine. *Families Apart: Migrant Mothers and the Conflicts of Labor and Love*. Minneapolis: University of Minnesota Press, 2012.

Private Practice. "Show Summary." http://www.tv.com/shows/private-practice/.

"Problematic Aspects in Ester Boserup's *Woman's Role in Economic Development*. http://www.africaresource.com/essays-a-reviews/gender/131-problematic-aspects-of-ester-boserups-womans-role-in-economic-development?showall=&start=3.

Quaicoe-Duho, Elsie. "Female MP in Ghana's First Republic shares her Experience—Calls for Peaceful Elections." Becce Quaicoe's Library, December 3, 2012. http://becceq7317.blogspot.com/2012/12/female-mp-in-ghana-first-republic.html.

Quinn, Joseph F, and Kevin E. Cahill. "The New World of Retirement Income Security in America" *American Psychologist* 71, no. 4 (2016): 321–333.

Refugee Adjudication Board. "*Owusu-Ansah v. Canada*. Minister of Employment and Immigration (1989). 8 Imm. L.R. (2d) 106 (F.C.A.).

———. *Karika*ri v. Canada. Minister of Employment and Immigration (1994). 159 N.R. 131 (F.C.A.).

Renzetti, Claire M., Daniel Curran and Shana Maier. *Women, Men, and Society*. Boston: Pearson, 2012.

Reynolds, Edward. "Ghana, Republic of: Acheampong Regime to the Third Republic, 1972–1981." In *Encyclopedia of African History,* edited by Kevin Shillington (London: Routledge, 2004). htpps://voyager.ship.edu/rpas/ezproxy.cgi?institution=15&url=http://search.credoreference.com/content/entry/routafricanhistory/ghana_republic_of_acheampong_regime_to_the_third_republic_1972_1981/0?institutionId=649.

Rio, Cecilia Marie. "This Job has no End:" African American Domestic Workers and Class Becoming. In *Class and its Others*, edited by J. K. Gibson-Graham, Stephen A. Resnick and Richard D. Wolff, 23–46. Minneapolis: University of Minnesota Press, 2000. ProQuest Ebook Central.

Robinson, Victoria, and Diane Richardson. *Introducing* Women's *and Gender Studies*. 4th ed. London: Palgrave, 2010.

Rodney, Walter. *How Europe Underdeveloped Africa*. London: Bogle-L'Ouverture Publications, 1972.

Rollins, Judith. *Between Women: Domestics and their Employers*. Philadelphia: Temple University Press, 1985.

Romero, Mary. *Maid in the USA*. New York: Routledge, 1992.

Sankofa. Profile of Great African History Maker -Dr. James Emmanuel Kwegyir Aggrey. December 2, 2016. http://sankofaonline.com/archives/9078.

———. Ghanaian Chicago Community. "How Many Excuses, Asiedu Nketia? NPP-USA Women's Wing." http://sankofaonline.com/archives/31101.

Sassen, Saskia. 1996. ''Beyond Sovereignty: Immigration Policy Making Today.'' Social Justice 23(3): 9–20.

———. 2004. ''Global Cities and Survival Circuits.'' In *Global Woman: Nannies, Maids, and Sex Workers in the New Economy*, edited by Barbara Ehrenreich and Arlie Russell Hochschild, 254–274. New York: Metropolitan Books.

———. "Economics II: Push Factors." *Encyclopedia of American Immigration* (2001): 265–276.

Schweizer, Peter A. *Survivors on the Gold Coast: The Basel Missionaries in Colonial Ghana*. Accra: Smartline Publishing, 2001.

Seyassa, Al. "Torture Disables Maid, Kuwait Couple Acquitted." *Kuwait Times,* March 19, 2017. http://www.timeskuwait.com/Times_Torture-disables-maid-Kuwaiti-couple-acquitted.

Serres, Chris. "Senior's Rape Throws Light on Problems in Assisted Living Homes." *Star Tribune*, March 27, 2014. http://www.startribune.com/senior-s-rape-throws-light-on-problems-in-assisted-living-homes/252567371/.

Sharpless, Rebecca. *Cooking in Other Women's Kitchens: Domestic Workers in the South, 1865–1960*. Chapel Hill, NC: University of North Carolina Press, 2010. E-Book.

Shillington, Kevin. *Ghana and the Rawlings Factor*. London: Macmillan, 1992.

Shiva, Vandana. "Our Violent Economy is hurting Women." In *Women in a Globalizing World: Transforming Equality, Development, Diversity and Peace,* edited by Angela Miles. Toronto: Inanna Publications and Education Inc., 2013.

Shu-Ju Ada Cheng. "Rethinking Differences and Inequality at the Age of Globalization: A Case Study of White Immigrant Domestic Workers in the Global City of Chicago." *Equality, Diversity and Inclusion: An International Journal* 32, no. 6 (2013): 537–556.

Sivard, Ruth Leger. *Women: A World Survey*. Washington, DC: World Priorities, 1995.

Slaughter, Anne Marie. "Why Women Still Can't have it All." *Atlantic Monthly*, July/August, 2012. https://www.theatlantic.com/magazine/archive/2012/07/why-women-still-cant-have-it-all/309020.

Ssenyonga, Allan Brian. "Americanization or Globalization." In *Taking Sides: Clashing Views on Global Issues*, edited by James E Harf and Michael O. Lombardi, 274–278. New York: McGraw-Hill, 2010.

Tetzlaff, Rainer. "World Cultures under the Pressure of Globalization: Experiences and Responses from the Different Continents." 2000. http://www.hamburgerblldungsserver.de/global/allgemein/tetzlaff-120.htm

Tong, Rosemarie. *Feminist Thought*, 4th ed. Boulder, CO.: Westview Press, 2014.

"Throwback Photos of Ghanaians being deported from Nigeria in 1983." http://www.tori.ng/news/5806/see-historic-pictures-of-ghanaians-leaving-nigeria.html.

Ungerson, Clare. *Policy is Personal: Sex, Gender and Informal Care*. London: Tavistock, 1987.

UNICEF. "Declaration of the Rights of the Child, 1959." https://www.unicef.org/malaysia/1959-Declaration-of-the-Rights-of-the-Child.pdf.

United Nations. *Universal Declaration of Human Rights*. http://www.un.org/en/universal-declaration-human-rights/index.html.

UNODC. "Human Trafficking." http://www.unodc.org/unodc/en/human-trafficking/what-is-human-trafficking.html.

US Census Bureau. American Community Survey, 2010. https://www.census.gov/prod/2012pubs/acs-19.pdf.

US Court of Appeal, First Circuit. *United States of America, Appellee v. Talal H. Alzanki, Defendant, Appellant*, No. 94-1645.

US Department of Labor. Labor Statistics, 2012 and 2014. https://www.dol.gov/.

Velasco, Pura. "Migrant Workers amidst Globalization." In *Women in a Globalizing World: Transforming Equality, Development, Diversity and Peace*, edited by Angela Miles, 284–291. Toronto: Inanna Publications and Education Inc., 2013.

Vellos, Diana. "Immigrant Latina Domestic Workers and Sexual Harassment." *American University Journal of Gender and the Law* 5, no. 2 (1997): 407–432.

Wanshel, Elyse. "Landscaper in Canada become King in Ghana, Still Mows Lawns." *Huffington Post*, September 29, 2016. http://www.huffingtonpost.com/entry/eric-manu-west-african-tribe-king-landscaper-canada-healthcare_us_57e153a1e4b04a1497b6ba2b.

Waters, Tony. "A Cultural Analysis of the Economy of Affection and the Uncaptured Peasantry in Tanzania." *Journal of Modern African Studies* 30, no. 1 (March 1992): 163–175.

WDRB. "In-home Caregiver Accused of Stealing Jewelry from Louisville Client." March 20, 2014. http://www.wdrb.com/story/25027370/in-home-caregiver-accused-of-stealing-jewelry-from-louisville-client.

Weir, Alison. "Global Care Chains: Freedom, Responsibility, and Solidarity." *The Southern Journal of Philosophy* 46 (2008): 166–175.

———. "The Global Universal Caregiver: Imagining Women's Liberation in the New Millennium." *Constellations: An International Journal of Critical and Democratic Theory* 12, no. 3 (September 2005): 308–330.

Whitfield, Lindsay. "Trustees of Development from Conditionality to Governance: Poverty Reduction Strategy Papers in Ghana." *The Journal of Modern African Studies* 43, no. 4 (Dec 2005): 641–664.

Wilson, Colwin M. and Leon C. Wilson. "Domestic Work in the United States of America: Past Perspectives and Future Directions," n.d. http://www.rcgd.isr.umich.edu/prba/perspectives/winter2000/cwilson.pdf.

Wilts, Teresa. "Growing African Immigrant Population is Highly Educated, Underemployed." The PEW Charitable Trusts, May 14, 2015. http://www.pewtrusts.org/en/research-and-analysis/blogs/stateline/2015/5/14/growing-african-immigrant-population-is-highly-educated-underemployed.

Wirth, Nicholaus. "Capitein, Jacobus Elisa Johannes (1717?-1747)." *BlackPast.org.* http://www.blackpast.org/gah/capitein-jacobus-elisa-johannes-1717-1747#sthash.XQu9OpMa.dpuf.

"Women in America: Indicators of Social and Economic Well-Being." U.S. Department of Commerce, Economics and Statistics Administration and the Executive Office of the President, Office of Management and Budget, for the White House Council on Women and Girls, March 2011.

World Bank. Sector Policy Paper, 1980. http://www.worldbank.org/.

Wrigley-Asante, Charlotte. "Survival or Escaping Poverty: The Perspectives of Poverty and Well-being among Ghanaian Women in Cross-border Trading." *Journal of Gender Studies* 22, no. 3 (2013): 320–334. http://dx.doi.org/10.1080/09589236.2012.703519.

Yahoo Newsroom. "Another Maid falls to her Death in Serangoon." May 18, 2012. https://sg.news.yahoo.com/another-maid-falls-to-her-death-in-serangoon.html.

Zaami, Mariama. "Experiences of Socio-Spatial Exclusion among Ghanaian Immigrant Youth in Toronto: A Case Study of the Jane-Finch Neighbourhood" (2012). *Electronic Thesis and Dissertation Repository.* Paper 604.

Zimmerman, Mary K., Jacquelyn S. Litt, and Christine E. Bose. *Global Dimensions of Gender and Carework.* Stanford, Calif.: Stanford Social Sciences, 2006.

Index

abuse, 9, 37, 48, 62–65, 71–74, 76, 78, 81–82, 90, 109, 119, 123;
of care recipients, 81–82
African American women, xii, 48–49, 52, 56–57, 83
Agege, 33. *See also* Nigeria
agency, women's, x–xii, xv, 23, 43, 49, 55–56, 66, 74, 102, 109, 119, 121
Aggrey, James Kwegyir, 32
Akan, 22–23, 63, 77, 80, 84, 89
Americanization, 2
Americanized, 110
Armed Forces Revolutionary Council, 18
Asante, 16, 21, 24

baby boomers, 50
borger, 40–41, 55, 62, 66, 86, 117
Britain (British), x, 2, 14–16, 23–24, 31–32

Canada, x, 36, 38–39, 40–41, 42–43, 54, 58
capitalism, x, 2, 87, 122
capitalist globalization, ix, 3–5, 49, 78, 120–21. *See also* globalization
Capitein, Jacobus, 32
care work, ix–xv, 8–9, 49–50, 52, 55, 58–59, 61–62, 64, 66, 73–76, 81, 83–86, 88–91, 95–96, 98–99, 119, 113–15, 119–23;
exploitation of women in, ix–xii, xv, 9, 37–38, 50, 71–72, 76, 85, 87, 89, 91, 109, 119, 120, 122–23;
invisibility in, 9, 72, 76, 104, 123;
isolation of women in, 9, 56, 64, 71–72, 74, 76–77, 90–91, 96;
undervaluation of, xi, xiv, 48, 71, 75, 104, 123
care workers, emotional attachment to work, 83–84;
spiritual satisfaction of work, 83–84
class shift, 99
colonialism, ix, 3–5, 20, 122;
globalization and, 4, 26, 120
colonization, of Africa, 15, 23, 26, 120
connection, 35–38, 41
coup d'état in Ghana, 13, 17, 21
cultural associations, 94, 104
cultural disconnect, 80, 81

Davidson, Basil, 15
domestic work (domestic workers), ix, xi–xii, xiv, 7–9, 47–49, 49, 51–53, 56–58, 72–76, 78, 82–85, 96, 101–2, 113, 122–23
double day (second shift), xi, xiii, 6–8, 95–96

economy of affection, 54
ECOWAS, 31
Ehrenreich, Barbara, 49–51, 73, 85, 93, 120
Elmina, 14

Fair Labor Standards Act, 76
family, types of, xiv;
accordion, 96;
diasporic, 97, 105;
hybridized, xiv, 97, 105;
transnational, 97
Filipino domestic workers, 73, 96, 99

Ghana, x;
global economy and, x, xiv, 6, 13–17, 20–21
globalization, xii, xiv, 26, 78, 122
market women in, 19, 23
women and politics in, 23, 26
Ghanaian immigrant community, 36, 56, 74, 103–5, 123;
churches in, 74, 104–5;
cultural associations in, 97, 104;
funerals in, 103–4, 106
Ghanaian women:
economic activities, 22–23, 26;
international migration, 31–32, 38–39;
politics, 23–26
globalization, ix–xv, 2–6, 10, 13, 26, 49, 78, 107, 120–22;
impact on Third World women, 49–50;
positive impact of, 3, 6
Gold Coast, 3, 14, 16, 22

Hochschild, Arlie Russell, 6–8, 49–51, 73, 85, 93, 110, 120
home ownership, 66, 117
Hondagneu-Sotelo, Pierrette, 79–80, 83
housework, remuneration for, 87–88
Human Rights Watch, 9, 73

IMF, 4–6, 20
immigrant care workers, x, xi, 86
Immigration and Naturalization Service (INS), 35
International Covenant on Civil and Political Rights, 61
international migration, 2, 13, 31–32, 38–39;
women and, 2, 13, 31–32, 38–39

kalabule, 17, 19
Katrina, Hurricane, 1

live-in, as escape, xiv, 47, 59–60
live-in as sanctuary, 47, 62, 65, 90
live-in caregivers:
performance of domestic chores, 65, 96, 102
relationship with husbands, 65, 98, 102–103, 112

Nakano-Glenn, Evelyn, 9
National Democratic Congress, 21
National Redemption Council, 17
Native Administrative Ordinance, 24
Nigeria, Ghanaian migration to, 15, 32–34, 40–41, 43, 74
Nkrumah, Kwame, 17, 32
NY State Department of Labor, 115

Parrenas, Rhacel Salazar, 86, 96, 99
patriarchal benevolence, ix, 50, 120
PDC (CDR), 19
play man women, 23, 55
PNDC, 19–20, 25
poverty, x, xii, xv, 17, 26, 39, 59, 115–16, 122
private practice, xi, xii, xiv, xv, 75–76, 78, 80, 81, 82, 85, 87, 113–14, 115, 117, 119, 120, 123

racism, domestic work and, xii, 48, 57–58, 66, 82
Rawlings, J. J., 6, 13, 17–21, 23, 25, 33–34, 38–39;
coup d'état of, 13, 17–19;
and IMF, 20;

and market women, 19–20;
and structural adjustment program, 21
Rawlings, Konadu Agyemang, 25
regressive thinking, 100
Rodney, Walter, 15

sacrificial love, 86
sanctuary, 90
structural adjustment programs, 4, 20–21, 38;
impact on women, 6, 21
structuration, theory of, 102
Supreme Military Council I and II, 17

trafficking, 36–37
transfer of affection, 86, 110
transnational corporations, 2–5;
negative impact on Third World countries, 3–6;
positive impact on Third World countries, 3
transnational family, 96, 116
triple management, xiv, 8, 96

UN Declaration of Human Rights, 34
UN Declaration on the Rights of the Child, 85
unemployment insurance, 114–15
UNHCR, 34
UN Human Rights Committee, 73
UN Office of Drugs and Crime, 36
US Department of Labor, 51, 85
US v. Alzanki, 73

West Germany, Ghanaian migration to, 34–35, 40
women of color, xii, 9, 48, 50, 53, 66, 120
work-family conflict, xiv, 95
World Bank, 4–6, 20

About the Author

Martha Donkor is associate professor of history and women's and gender studies at West Chester University of Pennsylvania. She was born in Ghana. She obtained her first degree in history from the University of Cape Coast and continued her education in Canada at the University of Guelph, obtaining an MA in American history and then a PhD in the history of immigrant women's education from the Ontario Institute for Studies in Education, University of Toronto. Dr. Donkor's research interests include African immigrant and refugee populations in North America, women and education, work, and poverty. She has done extensive work on the Ghanaian immigrant population in Canada, the most recent being a funded investigation into the causes of familial tension and disengagement between sponsored teenaged immigrants and their sponsors in Toronto. Dr. Donkor is also working on a book manuscript on defilement (girl) child rape in Ghana. She is the author of *Sudanese Refugees in the United States: The Collateral Damage of Sudan's Civil War*.

Lightning Source UK Ltd.
Milton Keynes UK
UKOW04n0742241117
313207UK00011B/556/P

9 781498 564458